THE NAMES
OF MAINE

THE NAMES
OF MAINE

HOW MAINE PLACES GOT THEIR NAMES

AND WHAT THEY MEAN

BRIAN MCCAULEY
With Illustrations by Matthew Dimock

ACADIA PRESS
Wellesley, Massachusetts

ACADIA PRESS
74 Elmwood Road,
Wellesley, Massachusetts 02481

www.acadia-press.com
www.thenamesofmaine.com

Cover painting and illustrations by Matthew Dimock

Design and layout by Jonathan Gullery

Library of Congress Cataloging-in-Publication Data available at
www.thenamesofmaine.com

ISBN 0-9740412-8-9

Printed in the United States of America

10 9 8 7 6 5 4 3 2 1

*For Annie, Sara, and Hannah
for their love and encouragement,
and
for my mom and dad, Barbara and Pat McCauley,
who gave me their love of exploring the shores,
hills, and mountains.*

N

CANADA

Madawaska

Van Buren

St. John River

Allagash River

Caribou

Presque Isle

Aroostook River

Eagle Lake

CANADA

Chesuncook Lake

Houlton

Mt. Katahdin

95

Moosehead Lake

Jackman

Millinocket

Kennebec River

St. Croix River

Lincoln

Maine

Calais

Penobscot River

Rangeley

Madison

Eastport

Skowhegan

95

Bangor

NEW HAMPSHIRE

Waterville

Ellsworth

Androscoggin River

Bethel

Bar Harbor

Augusta ⊗

Camden

Acadia Nat'l Park

Harrison

Lewiston

Bath

Isle au Haut

Brunswick

Portland

Saco

Monhegan Island

Atlantic Ocean

Sanford

Biddeford

Kennebunkport

York

Kittery

0   40 mi

© Karen Schneider 2004

CONTENTS

INTRODUCTION

I first visited Maine in the summer of 1977 when I worked as a counselor at a boys' summer camp leading trips. I explored every part of the state and, like millions of others, fell in love with Maine's beauty and culture. I also became fascinated by the place names. Who wouldn't? Acadia, Moosehead, Aroostook, Blue Hill, Penobscot, Passamaquoddy, Monhegan, Kennebunk, Wiscasset…the list goes on and on. Since then, I have continued to explore Maine: by canoe on the Allagash, St. John, St. Croix, Sheepscot, and Androscoggin Rivers; by foot, hiking many miles and climbing Mt. Katahdin, both in the sunshine and when the rain was blown horizontally as we crossed the Knife's Edge; by sailboat, cruising much of the coastline and exploring many islands; and by car, driving thousands of miles throughout the state. Everywhere I've gone, the names of Maine have captivated me and nine years ago I began to look into where they came from and what they mean.

The study of place names is called toponymy, from the Greek words "topo" meaning "place" and "onym" meaning "word" or "name." Some toponymy is etymological, but the toponymy of Maine is usually not. Maine place names typically fit into the following categories: Native American names; descriptive names of geographic features, plants, or animals; honorific names, which are named after early settlers, landowners and their relatives, or famous people; transplanted names, mostly from England, but also from other foreign places; and cultural sources such as Biblical names or names from literature.

Place name authorities have a rule of thumb that there is a place name for about every square mile. That would suggest that there are over 33,000 place names in Maine. This book covers over 1,000 names including all of the cities and towns and the larger rivers, lakes, mountains, bays, and islands.

This book is not so much an original work as it is a gathering together of many pieces of information found in numerous places. Much of the research was done at the Boston Athenaeum, which has an excellent collection on Maine. In the 1800s and early 1900s, many histories of Maine towns and areas were written, the collected speeches of centennial celebrations were published, and record books were printed. I am indebted to the many men and women who, usually long ago, wrote thorough histories of their towns and regions. Most contain valuable information about how the sites were named, who early settlers were, and other items of interest, such as important dates. Additionally, I read numerous other books, articles, and descriptions of Maine, many of them providing important information about how and when places were named. There are several helpful books that explain the Native American names. I consulted over 150 books and a bibliography is on this book's web site (www.thenamesofmaine.com).

Different sources sometimes give differing information about names. Usually all opinions are presented in this book. There are inevitable mistakes in a work such as this; sources may have had bad information, or I may have misinterpreted information. Any mistakes are the fault of the author alone. If the reader has information to correct any errors or additional information for future editions, please contact me. This book is not intended to be a scholarly work, but was written for everyone who wants to know more about Maine.

I also include a very short history of Maine to help the reader know more about Maine's fascinating history, and to understand the context of how places were named. Most people are unaware of how Maine was discovered, explored, parceled out, settled and governed, including the fact that Maine was part of Massachusetts until 1820. This brief history will give those with little knowledge, or who need a refresher, the historical perspective to enjoy this book more fully.

There are many interesting aspects to toponymy that are beyond the scope of this book. The experts see patterns based on when sites were named and on settlement patterns. For example, if you draw a line across Maine at approximately the latitude of Bangor, you will find a huge difference in the use of the adjectives "great" (i.e. Great Diamond Island) and "big" (i.e. Big Island) as the first word in a place name. Ninety-five percent of all "greats" are below the line, while eighty-two percent of all "bigs" are above it. This reflects a change in the use of language over time or a change in where settlers came from, as places north of the line were settled much later than those south of it—typically after 1800. There is a similar line a little farther south of Bangor. The suffix "burg" is used frequently south of that line and "boro" is used north of it. This book does not examine such issues, but limits itself to the source of the names, their meaning, and some history about the place.

Writing this book has been a wonderful experience, particularly all the time logged in Maine, but also the time researching in libraries and writing at the computer. There are several books I have particularly enjoyed and would like to mention in case the reader might enjoy them, too. Bill Caldwell's *Islands of Maine, Where America Really Began* is a well-written, interesting account of the history of Maine's islands, crafted by a man who sailed among them for many years. *Monhegan, The Cradle of New England*, by Ida Sedgwick Proper, tells the fascinating story of the discovery and exploration of New England and Monhegan Island. It was published in 1930 and will be harder to find, but is a very compelling account of who may have been to New England long before Columbus' time. Christopher J. Lenny wrote an intriguing book called *Sightseeking, Clues to the Landscape History of New England*. This book is unique in that it gives the reader a new perspective of the history and patterns of place names, roads, architecture, language, gravestones, and other social and cultural elements. You will never think about or view New England the same way again after having your eyes opened to the physical and cultural landscape the way this book does.

Stone walls are one of the best things about New England. Robert M. Thorson tells everything about them in his wonderful book, *Stone By Stone, The Magnificent History in New England's Stone Walls*. Since cod was the silver that made Maine and the rest of New England rich, along with timber and trade, Mark Kurlansky's book, *Cod, A Biography of the Fish That Changed the World* is enormously interesting. Maine, other parts of New England, and the Canadian Maritime Provinces wouldn't be what they are without cod and this book explains why. One last favorite is Samuel Eliot Morison's, *The Story of Mount Desert Island*. America's premier maritime historian writes about one of the most beautiful places on earth. Lastly, the Maine Historical Society has a wonderful library, museum, and other resources.

I highly recommend visiting them and becoming a member. It is at 485 Congress Street in Portland, and the phone number is 207-774-1822

May these pages add to your enjoyment and understanding of Maine!

MAINE FACTS

LAND

Land Area: 33,215 square miles, 380 miles long and 200 miles wide

Geographic Center: 18 miles north of Dover-Foxcroft in Piscataquis County

Number of counties: 16

Acres of forestland: 17 million

Number of lakes and ponds: 6,000

Miles of rivers and streams: 32,000

Number of rivers and streams: 5,100

Number of coastal islands: Over 2,000

Acres of State and National parks: 542,629

Percentage of Federally owned land: 0.872%

Largest county by land area: Aroostook, 6,672 square miles

Largest county by population: Cumberland, 267,000 people

Smallest county by land area: Sagadahoc, 254 square miles

Smallest county by population: Piscataquis, 17,000 people

Miles of coastline: 228 as the crow flies

Miles of shoreline: 3,500, about the same as California

Highest point on entire Atlantic coast: Cadillac Mountain, 1,530 feet

Highest point in Maine: Mt. Katahdin, 5,268 feet

Lowest point in Maine: Sea level

Easternmost point in 48 states: West Quoddy Head
Easternmost town in 48 states: Lubec

POPULATION

Population: Just under 1.3 million, ranks 40th in U.S.
Largest City: Portland, 64,250 people
Percentage of population that is white: 96.9%
Percentage African American: 0.05%
Percentage Hispanic: 0.07%
Native Americans in Maine: About 7,000
Number of people per square mile: 40

STATE

Statehood: March 15, 1820, the 23rd state
America's first legally recognized city: York, first called
    Gorgeana, in 1642
State Capital: Augusta
Average winter temperature: 22° F.
Average summer temperature: 70° F.
Highest recorded temperature: 107° F, North Bridgton, July
    10, 1911
Lowest recorded temperature: -48° F, Van Buren, January 19,
    1925
Average snowfall: Between 60 and 90 inches
Pounds of lobster harvested per year: About 57 million
Pounds of finfish harvested per year: About 128 million
Value of commercial fishing: About $270 million
Primary crops: Potatoes, aquaculture

Primary manufactured goods: paper and wood products,
   transportation equipment
Number of lighthouses: 71
Nickname: The Pine Tree State
State motto: *Dirigo*, Latin for "I lead"
State tree: White Pine
State animal: Moose
State flower: White Pine cone
State bird: Chickadee
State berry: Wild blueberry
State fish: Landlocked salmon
State cat: Maine Coon Cat
State insect: Honeybee
State herb: Wintergreen

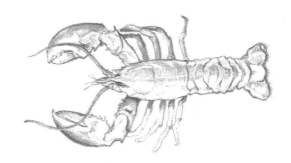

UNDATED MAP THOUGHT TO BE FROM THE 1630S.
COURTESY OF THE MAINE STATE ARCHIVES

A Very Short History of Maine

Pre-European Maine

Sixteen thousand years ago, a visitor to any part of Maine would have stood on an ice sheet 6,000 feet thick. It reached almost as far south into the Gulf of Maine as Cape Cod. The same ice sheet covered much of England and its impact as it withdrew was similar on both places. The geologist Robert Thorson writes, "In terms of the natural scenery, a journey from the English Lake District, near the border with Scotland, to the cliffs of Dover, opposite France, resembles one from the White Mountains of New Hampshire to Chatham, Cape Cod." Future settlers from England would find much about the New England landscape to be like home.

As the ice retreated north of the present coastline, the sea level rose and salt water flowed into the low valleys such as the Penobscot and Kennebec, where marine fossils can be found as far north as Bingham and Millinocket today. Thirteen thousand years ago, Maine was ice-free and soils began to form. Over the next several thousand years, plants and trees grew and animal life migrated in.

The first humans came to Maine about 11,500 years ago. Several different groups, known as Paleo Indians, Red Paint

People, Susquehannas, and the Ceramic Group came and left. By the time the first Europeans appeared, the major tribes of Maine were the Sacos, the Abenakis (which means "People of the Dawn"), and the Etechemins, all of the Algonquin stock. Each had numerous bands with their own names. The English named them after the rivers or other geographic features they lived near, hence the Penobscots, Passamaquoddys, etc. Their languages are similar, but the same word can have an entirely different meaning between the Abenakis and the Micmacs. An estimated 30,000 Indians lived in New England in 1600, including about 3,000 Abenakis in Maine, before many were wiped out by disease in the early 1600s.

EUROPEAN EXPLORATION

No one is certain when the first Europeans visited the shores of North America, but it is virtually certain that they arrived before Columbus landed in 1492. Inscriptions on a rock on Manana Island in Monhegan Harbor are believed to be Phoenician reading, "Ships from Phoenecia. Cargo platform." In the sixth century, St. Brendan of Ireland wrote about a journey he made that some historians think may have brought him to North America. The Norsemen made it to Newfoundland around the year 1000, and many scholars who have read their sagas about their trips and compared them to current maps feel certain that they visited the coast of Maine and stayed for several years in Massachusetts. An authenticated rare Norse coin was found in an archeological dig near the town of Brooklin, Maine.

In the late 1300s, the Zeni Brothers of Italy undertook explorations and made a map based on their voyages and knowledge that put parts of New England and Maritime Canada in realistic positions. Andrea Bianco drew a map in 1436 that shows an island where Newfoundland is called Stoxafixa. Stockfish is still a common name for codfish. Fishermen are notorious for keeping secrets and do not write about their prized fishing holes. However, some historians feel that Basque, Irish, and other European fishermen fished for cod off of Canada and Maine long before Columbus set sail, and that they used some of the islands for seasonal settlements and to dry the cod on the rocks and on wooden racks. Some writers think that Columbus heard fishermen on the docks of Bristol, England talking about the land across the ocean where fish were abundant. There is too much evidence not to think that a number of Europeans visited North America, including Maine, long before Columbus arrived.

The kings and queens of Europe, wanting to claim the riches of the New World and to find a route through or around the New World to the Orient, sent explorers to North America. Sebastian Cabot, an Italian sailing for England, probably explored Maine in 1498. The Portuguese Gaspar Cortereal seems to have sailed along the coast of Maine in 1500 looking for the elusive Northwest Passage. Giovanni de Verrazano, sailing for France, made an extensive exploration of Maine's coast in 1524. On his map, he labeled the area now known as the upper Penobscot "Oranbega."

The Spanish stranded David Ingram and two other Englishmen in Mexico in 1568. They walked from Mexico to New Brunswick, Canada, arriving in 1571, an epic journey. Picked up by a fishing vessel and returned to England, Ingram told tales of a city in Maine called Norumbega that was full of gold and pearls. After that, explorers of the northern latitudes hoped to find riches equal to those found by the Spanish in

South and Central America. Norumbega became the El Dorado of the North and was the pursuit of many until Champlain sailed up the Penobscot River in 1604 to about where Bangor sits today. There, he found a simple Indian village, debunking the myth of a City of Gold in Maine.

The area continued to be called Norumbega into the 1600s when the name "Maine" became more prevalent. In 1525, Estevan Gomez, a Spaniard, explored Maine and named several sites such as Saco Bay (Bahia de Saco) and Casco Bay (Bahia de Casco). Several more explorers sailed along the coast of Maine during the 1500s, but in the final years of Queen Elizabeth's reign—the end of the 1500s and the first several years of the 1600s—interest in what the English called Virginia increased significantly. Both England and France sent expeditions to solidify their claims to this area. Bartholomew Gosnold, Martin Pring, and George Weymouth made separate, detailed explorations of the Maine coast for England between 1602 and 1606, giving many names to places.

EUROPEAN SETTLEMENT

America began on the islands of Maine. Before settlements such as Jamestown were established, European fishermen were using islands such as Monhegan, Damariscove, and the Isles of Shoals as bases for fishing and fur trading. No gold or silver was found in Maine as they were in South America, but fortunes were made in another type of silver: cod. Long before the Pilgrims or Puritans arrived, men were sailing back and forth across the Atlantic, bringing dried cod and furs to a Europe hungry for both. By the time the Pilgrims disembarked at Plymouth, the coast of New England was well known and well mapped.

The English referred to America as Virginia in honor of

Elizabeth, the Virgin Queen (1533-1603). The mid-Atlantic region, including the State of Virginia, was known as Southern Virginia and what is called New England was Northern Virginia. The French called the northern areas "La Cadie," which probably came from the Indian word "quoddy" meaning "place." "La Cadie" later evolved into "Acadia." America had gained its name in 1507 from a mapmaker named Martin Waldseemuller, who called the new continent America after Amerigo Vespucci, an explorer given to exaggeration.

In 1604, after several unsuccessful attempts to establish colonies along the St. Lawrence, King Henry IV of France granted a charter stretching from about New Jersey to Cape Breton Island to Pierre du Guast, Sieur De Monts. He assembled a group of men, which included Samuel de Champlain, and they set sail for North America where they built a settlement on an island in the St. Croix River. Champlain did further exploring, discovering Mount Desert Island. He sailed up the Penobscot River looking for the fabled Norumbega, only to find a simple Indian village. Winter brutalized the men, so that in the spring they abandoned the settlement, moving it to today's Port Royal.

In 1606, King James I granted a charter for Virginia to a group of merchants from London and Plymouth who formed two companies. The London Company's charter stretched from approximately the South Carolina/North Carolina border to New York and the Plymouth Company's charter from about Washington D.C. to today's Maine/Canada border. The London Company established Jamestown in 1607, and that same year the Plymouth Company founded a settlement at the mouth of the Kennebec River under the command of Captain George Popham. Like the French, they found the winter too harsh, returning home in the spring. Some of them sailed in the

Virginia, a ship they had built that winter. It was the first ship built by Europeans in the New World.

One of the leading proprietors of the Plymouth Company was Sir Ferdinando Gorges. Despite his Latin sounding name, Gorges' family had been in England for centuries, and he was a favorite of Queen Elizabeth. Not discouraged by the failure of the Popham Colony, he plotted ways to realize the potential of their charter. In 1614, Captain John Smith explored Massachusetts and Maine and published a book about his travels in 1616 entitled *A Description of New England.* Smith was the first to use the term New England rather than North Virginia, and it was soon in common use. The Plymouth Company sent ships to New England, primarily to Damariscove and Monhegan Islands, each year for fish and furs.

In 1620, Gorges and others were granted a new charter under the title of The Council for New England, giving them a monopoly on fishing and trade from about Philadelphia to Newfoundland and from "sea to sea." The Pilgrims were given a grant for land south of the Hudson River in 1620, but landed at Provincetown and then sailed to Plymouth where they settled. Later, they received a grant for that area and in 1629 were given land up the Kennebec River for fur trading purposes.

In 1622, John Mason secured a grant from Cape Ann to the north. Later that same year, Mason and Gorges were granted the land from three miles north of the Merrimac River to the Kennebec River. In 1629, Mason and Gorges decided to split their grants and Mason took the land from the Merrimac River to the Piscataqua River and called it New Hampshire, as he was from Hampshire, England. This split determined New Hampshire's southern boundaries. Gorges claimed the land from the Piscataqua to the Kennebec. Many smaller grants were given during the 1620s and 30s, including the Muscongus grant, which became the Waldo Patent, the Lygonia Patent (named after his mother whose maiden name was Lygon), several Kennebec patents, and the Pemaquid Patent.

The English long had disputed the French claims to the area from Penobscot Bay east. During skirmishes over the years, the English destroyed several settlements including one near the present site of Southwest Harbor on Mount Desert Island. Relationships between England and France improved over time, and in 1632 King Charles I, who had married the sister of Louis XIII, gave Acadia to France, though they continued to dispute whether the boundary was the Penobscot River or the Kennebec River. In 1635, Gorges dissolved The Council for New England, and the King gave him a new grant from the Piscataqua to the Kennebec, which Gorges called New Somersetshire, Somerset being the part of England he was from. He had complete power over the entire area, as if he were a feudal lord.

Gorges received another charter in 1639 for the Province of Maine. It states that the area, "shall forever be called the Province and County of Maine and not by any other name whatsoever." This appears to be the first use of the name Maine in an official document. In 1642, Gorges granted a charter for the first city in America, which he called Gorgeana after himself. Gorges died in 1647 having never visited Maine and spending much of his fortune on trying to develop it into a successful venture. He should be known as the Father of Maine, as no one did more to promote the settlement and development of Maine in the early days than he did. Regrettably, the only site to bear his name today is old, run-down Fort Gorges in Casco Bay.

Gorges' heirs did virtually nothing regarding Maine for several years. In 1652, Massachusetts, having grown much more rapidly than the areas to the north, sent representatives from the General Court, their governing body, to claim New Hampshire and Maine for Massachusetts. Over the next several years, all of the patents west of the Presumpscot River submitted to Massachusetts. Massachusetts promptly renamed Gorgeana, York and Maine, Yorkshire. Gorges' heirs later appealed to King Charles II, and in 1660 he ruled that the Province of Maine belonged to them and not to Massachusetts. He also restored New Hampshire to Mason's heirs. Massachusetts bought Maine from Sir Ferdinando Gorges' grandson for 1,250 pounds in 1678. Between 1680 and 1690, control of Maine shifted between Massachusetts and the Crown, until 1691 when William and Mary granted a new charter to Massachusetts whose rule was established in the General Court. Maine became the District of Maine, a part of Massachusetts, and was also governed by the General Court.

THE FOUR INDIAN WARS AND THE FRENCH AND INDIAN WAR

France continued to control Acadia, though there were frequent skirmishes with the British until 1713 when the Treaty of Utrecht ended the European war between England and France. England received Acadia as part of the agreement. Fewer than 1,000 settlers were living in Acadia at the time, and only a few thousand were living in Southern Maine. A series of four wars with the Indians had begun in 1675 with King Phillip's War. It was followed by King William's War from 1678 to 1698, Queen Anne's War from 1703 to 1711, and Lovewell's War from 1723 to 1725. These wars drove most of the few settlers there were from Maine, and new settlement didn't begin in earnest until the end of hostilities. Fishermen continued to fish from bases on the islands, but the Indians occasionally attacked there as well. The line between New Hampshire and Maine north of the Piscataqua River was in dispute for many years, and the King fixed the line in 1739. Massachusetts encouraged settlement in Maine by giving or selling land to settlers or to proprietors willing to settle families and establish churches, schools, and businesses. The peopling of Maine began to accelerate.

When in 1744, France declared war on England, Massachusetts voted to send an expedition against the French fort at Louisbourg, France's stronghold at the mouth of the St. Lawrence River. Three thousand men responded to the call under the command of William Pepperell of Kittery, Maine. In an exciting siege, they took the fort, earning Pepperell a knighthood for his success. However, the Treaty of Aix-la-Chapelle ending the war gave Louisbourg back to France. The colonists were outraged by the British action, but now realized that they could fight on their own without British troops, if need be. When the French and Indian War ended with the Treaty of Paris in 1763, the French had no more claims in New England, Newfoundland, or Canada except for several small islands off Newfoundland. Many of the French, known as Acadians, left these areas and went to French Louisiana. There, the word Acadian changed over time, becoming the word "Cajun."

THE REVOLUTIONARY WAR

As new settlers continued to come to Maine, the primary means of making a living were fishing, farming, trading, ship building, lumbering, land development, shop keeping, and several other trades. Roads were minimal and most transportation was by water up and down the coast. The population grew from about 15,000 in the 1750s, to 24,000 in 1764, to 96,500 in 1790, to almost 229,000 in 1810. During the 1760s and early 1770s, many colonists in Maine were troubled by the British actions to tax the colonies, such as the Stamp Act and the Townsend Acts. Some in Maine were loyalists to the King, but many supported independence.

The first naval battle of the Revolution was June 11, 1775, when men from Maine captured the British ship *Margueritta* near Machias. This was the first time the Union Jack was struck to Americans. On October 17, after months of resistance by the people of Falmouth (today's Portland), four British ships bombarded the city all day and then sent parties ashore to burn as many buildings as they could, destroying two-thirds of the town. News of Falmouth's destruction inflamed Americans and helped fuel their resolve to become independent. Maine men fought at Bunker Hill, were part of the siege of Boston, wintered at Valley Forge, and served with Benedict Arnold on his epic march up the Kennebec and through the northern wilds of Maine during the winter to try to capture Quebec. Maine ship builders played key roles in the naval battles of Lake Champlain.

SETTLEMENT AFTER THE WAR

The Revolution left the states with large debts, and Massachusetts was no exception. The General Court made a plan to sell land in Maine to help retire the debt, but there were few sales and they were on a small scale until General Henry Knox decided to get involved. He and several colleagues bought 2 million acres: one million on the Kennebec River and another million west of the Penobscot River. They put $10,000 down on a sale worth over $400,000. Needing more money, Knox talked to his old friend William Bingham of Philadelphia, a future

Senator who had been a major financier of the War. Bingham bought the land, agreeing to share some profits with Knox, and the sale has been known since as the Bingham Purchase. However, it was difficult to get settlers to move to Maine and Bingham's sales were slow. Most settlers just squatted on the land. When Bingham died in 1807, his heirs almost lost the land through legal maneuvering, but after they paid off William King—the main figure trying to nullify their purchase—they held on to their land.

THE 19TH CENTURY

As more and more people moved to Maine during the late 1700s and early 1800s, the people of Maine began discussing separation from Massachusetts. Conventions were held in Falmouth in 1785 and again in 1786 to consider separation. Maine was becoming stronger and more independent, enjoying the fruits of its growth industries such as ship building, trading, and farming. Unfortunately, another war was looming. Since the sea was the primary economic force in Maine, Britain's seizure of American ships and the impressment of American sailors was very unpopular. However, like all of New England, the people of Maine resisted going to war with Britain, though to no avail.

Once the War of 1812 started, a number of Maine vessels became privateers and took many prize ships and cargoes from British ships. One of the most successful was the *Dash*, built by the Porter Brothers at Porters Landing in Freeport. The British occupied most of Maine from the Penobscot River to Eastport. In a significant naval battle fought between the HM Brig *Boxer* and the USS *Enterprise*, the *Enterprise* won, though both captains were killed in the battle. They were later buried side by side on Munjoy's Hill in Portland.

When the war ended, the British refused to leave the eastern part of Maine. The people of Maine asked the governor of Massachusetts to send the militia just as they had during the war, but he refused, fueling separation fever once again. In 1816, a separation law was defeated, but another passed in 1819 and Maine became the twenty-third state on March 15, 1820 as part of the Missouri Compromise. Maine was admitted as a free state and Missouri as a slave state to keep the balance between free and slave states. Maine was almost called the State of Columbia, but the name was voted down as people might confuse it with the Columbia River or the country in South America. Portland became the first capital until 1832 when the capital was moved to Augusta.

Since the end of the Revolution, Maine and Canada had disputed the northeastern boundary between Maine and New Brunswick. In 1839, Governor John Fairfield sent two hundred men who arrested twenty Canadians in the disputed area, but they were in turn captured by a group of Canadians and put in jail. The Maine Legislature sent the militia and the British moved troops to the area. No shots were fired, and in 1842 Daniel Webster and Lord Ashburton negotiated a treaty setting the current borders, ending the Aroostook War.

The 1840s and 50s saw commerce continue to expand. Trade, shipbuilding, and lumbering grew rapidly. The significant issues in Maine were the abolition of slavery, prohibition, and strong feelings of discrimination against certain immigrant groups, particularly Roman Catholics. When the Civil War began, Maine sent over 72,000 men to the Union Army. Over 7,000 men from Maine died and monuments to those killed can be found in most Maine towns. General Joshua Chamberlain, the most famous Mainer of the War, commanded the Twentieth Maine at Little Big Top where a Confederate flanking move was repulsed during the Battle of Gettysburg. He won the Medal of Honor for his bravery that day and later accepted Robert E. Lee's sword when he surrendered at Appomattox. He went on to become governor of Maine and president of Bowdoin College.

The rest of the century saw railroads built throughout Maine, improving transportation significantly. Many mills were constructed along rivers to capitalize on the waterpower, giving manufacturing a boost. Wealthy people from New York, Philadelphia, Boston, and other areas found summertime in Maine to be to their liking, and many bought land and built large summer homes, calling themselves "rusticators."

When the Spanish-American War began, many Maine men volunteered. The sinking of the battleship Maine in Havana Harbor caused the rallying cry of the war, "Remember the Maine." When the ship was later raised, the silver service was presented to the state and is used at the Governor's residence in Augusta.

THE 20TH CENTURY

The new century saw rapid progress in Maine. Over 35,000 men and women from Maine served in the First World War. When hydroelectricity became a significant issue early in the century, the state voted to ban sales of hydroelectric power outside of the state, hoping industry would move to Maine. As the Depression was particularly hard on Maine, especially in the rural areas, its typically Republican electorate sided with the Democrats in 1932 and 1934, coming back to the Republicans for several decades after those two elections. Almost 100,000 men and women from Maine served in World War II. In 1948,

Congresswoman Margaret Chase Smith became the first Republican woman elected to the U.S. Senate. Edmund Muskie was elected governor as a Democrat in 1954, went on to the Senate, and was a national political figure who ran for president in 1972. Road construction increased after the war, and automobile travel grew rapidly, while maritime travel decreased. This, along with many other factors, caused an increase in tourism throughout the remainder of the century, making tourism one of Maine's most important industries. Between 1931 and 1962, Percival Baxter, a former governor, purchased 202,000 acres of wilderness around Mt. Katahdin and presented the land to the State to be preserved "forever wild" as a state park. Since then, Maine has developed a strong environmental ethic, doing much to protect its forests, waters, and shoreline. Maine's politics have become increasingly independent to liberal, and in 2004 Maine has a Democrat governor, two Republican Senators, and two Democrat Congressmen.

THE NAMES
OF MAINE

A

Abbot Village: One of several towns granted by the General Court to Bowdoin College in 1794. John Abbott, a Harvard educated professor and the college's treasurer, sold parcels of the land to settlers to generate revenue for the college. Named for him in 1827.

Acadia: In 1603, King Henry IV of France granted a charter to Pierre du Guast, Sieur de Monts for the lands between the 40th and 46th parallels, roughly from today's Philadelphia to the mouth of the St. Lawrence. The land being granted was called "La Cadie." In reality, de Monts viewed his grant as being from Penobscot Bay up to the St. Lawrence. There are several theories about the origin of the name. Some say it comes from the Abenaki or Micmac word "quoddy" meaning "place." One thought is that it comes from the "aquoddy" in Passamaquoddy. Verrazano likely gave this name to the area when he visited Maine waters while exploring for the King of France in 1524. Another theory is that it comes from the ancient Greek Arcadia. As Mt. Desert Island became a popular destination for the well to do in the late 1800s, George B. Dorr and others worked to save as much land as possible for public use. They obtained 6,000 acres by 1913 and in 1916 the Federal Government established Sieur de Monts National Monument. In 1919 the name was changed to Lafayette National Park to honor the Marquis de Lafayette who was so instrumental in helping gain America's freedom during the Revolution. It was the first National Park east of the Mississippi River. The name was changed to Acadia National Park in 1929 because the owner of a large plot of land on the Schoodic Peninsula was willing to give their land to the park, but only on the condition that the name be changed, as they were not fond of things French. Today the park encompasses 35,000 acres.

Acton: First settled in 1776, the area was first called Hubbardstown, after many settlers with that name, and was incorporated as Acton in 1830 to honor the town of Acton where a battle of the Revolutionary War was fought. It was named after an English town that is now a part of London.

Addison: Named after Joseph Addison, a popular English writer in 1797. First settled around 1779, it was originally called Pleasant River and then Englishman's River.

Agamenticus: This is the Abenaki name for today's York. The name means "the little river which hides behind an island in its mouth." The name is now connected to a mountain and other features north of York, which have no connection to the original meaning that came from the river.

Alamoosook Lake: Anglicized Malecite meaning "at the fish spawning place."

Albion: Settled sometime before 1790, it was named Albion in 1824 after the ancient name of England.

Alexander: One of two towns named for Alexander Baring, Lord Ashburton, of England in 1825. In 1842, Baring, as British Ambassador, and Daniel Webster, the Secretary of State, settled the dispute over the northeastern boundary of Maine.

Alfred: The first settler came to the area in 1764 and in 1794 it was named after the ninth century English King, Alfred the Great. The oldest continuous court records in the U.S. are in the Alfred courthouse. The Indian name for the area was Massabesic.

Allagash: Abenaki for "bark cabin" or "bark place."

Allen Island: Alexander Allen owned the island during the Revolution.

Allens Mills: First settled around 1793, it was named for the Allen family in 1823.

Alligator Lake: Named for the shape of the lake.

Alna: Originally called New Milford after the mills on the river, many residents wanted a better name. In 1811, they selected Alna from the Latin *alnus* for "alder," since many alder trees grew along the river.

Alton: Probably named for Alton, Southampton, England.

Amesbury Point: Named for Edwin Amesbury, a sea captain.

Amherst: First settled around 1805, the town was named in 1831 after Amherst, New Hampshire, which was named for Lord Jeffrey Amherst, who came to America in 1758 and was governor-general of the British possessions in North America from 1760 to 1763.

Andover: The early settlers came from Old Andover, Massachusetts around 1789 and they called it East Andover to distinguish it from their old home. The "East" was dropped in 1821 after Maine became a separate state.

Andrews Island: Captain Stephen Andrews traded along the coast.

Androscoggin: Abenaki for "the place fish are cured." One historian thinks the first part of the name is an intentional slur of Governor Edmund Andros' name. He was a disliked royal governor of Massachusetts. The Abenaki word for fish is "ahmays" and "cogin" means cure. Androscoggin County was created in 1854 and named after the river.

Annabesacook: Abenaki for "smooth water at outlet."

Anson: Named after Lord George Anson of England in 1798. North Anson split off from Anson in 1845, but they reunited in 1855. It was first settled around 1772. Major John Moor, a veteran of the Battle of Bunker Hill, was the first settler, building several mills in the area.

Appledore Island: Named for Appledore, England.

Appleton: Samuel Appleton of Ipswich, New Hampshire and several other young men settled this town in 1788.

Argyle: Scotland's Argyle County is the source of this town's name. First settled around 1810.

Aroostook: Micmac for "shallow river" or "beautiful river." The river is a branch of the St. John's River. The county was established in 1839 from parts of Washington County and Penobscot County. Later, land was added from Piscataquis and Somerset Counties. The county was initially settled by French Acadians from Nova Scotia and by people from Massachusetts.

Arrowsic: Abenaki for "place of obstruction." A legend says that an Indian dying of a poisoned arrow at this spot said, "I am arrow sick."

Arundel: The cape and other features are named for Lord Arundel of England.

Ash: The point and island near Owl'sHead are named for ash trees.

Ashland: Named after Henry Clay's estate in Kentucky. First called Ashland, the name was changed to Dalton to honor its first settler, and then back to Ashland.

Ashville: Benjamin Ash, an early settler, gave the town its name.

Athens: The capital of Greece was the source of this name. The area saw its first settlers in 1782.

Atlantic: Named for the ocean it sits by.

Attean: An Indian mispronunciation of Etienne Orson's first name. Orson was a settler in the area around 1793.

Auburn: There are two possible sources for this name: Goldsmith's poem "Sweet Auburn, loveliest village of the plain" or Aubourn, England.

Augusta: First known as Koussinock or Cushnoc, which means "there is current above" or "place above the tide" in Abenaki or Old Norse. This was the site of an early trading post. By 1675, there were people in the area, but frequent Indian battles kept settlers away until the mid 1700s. In 1713, a stone fort was built. Destroyed by Indians, a wooden fort called Fort Western was built in 1754. There were three families in the area by 1770 and it was incorporated in 1797. Augusta is named for Pamela Augusta Dearborn, daughter of General Henry Dearborn of Revolutionary War fame.

state capital in the 1800s

Aurora: Originally called Hampton, Aurora is named after the Greek goddess of dawn. It was settled in 1805 and incorporated in 1831.

Austin: These ponds and streams are named for the Austin family that settled in the area.

Avon: The early settlers thought the beauty of the rivers and mountains were similar to England's Shakespearean region of Avon. First settled around 1784.

Aziscohos: Abenaki for "small pine trees."

B

Babbidge Island: Named either for William Babbidge, an early settler, or a sea captain of that name.

Bailey Island: Named after Deacon Timothy Bailey who settled there in the mid 1700s.

Bagaduce: Micmac for "large tidewater stream."

Baker: There are a number of lakes and ponds with this name. If they are not named for settlers named Baker, the origin is unknown.

Bald: A descriptive name for Bald Head, Bald Point, several Bald Mountains, and Bald Mountain Pond. Usually implies a treeless, often rocky location.

Baldwin: Loammi Baldwin was an early landowner. The town was originally called Flintstown after Captain John Flint, whose company from Concord, Massachusetts was granted the land for their service in the Revolutionary War.

Ballastone Ledges: Area stones were used as ballast in ships.

Bancroft: Named for George Bancroft, a historian. First settled around 1830.

Bangor: Originally known as Conduskeag, the first settlers arrived about 1769. The residents first wanted the town to be called Sunbury, but the General Court did not grant this name. In 1790, the Reverend Seth Noble sailed to Boston and presented a petition to incorporate with the name Bangor. This was the name of one of his favorite hymns and his petition was granted.

Bangs Island: Named for Joshua Bangs, who also owned Cushing Island for a while.

Bar Harbor: Named after Bar Island, which is in the harbor. Bar is descriptive for the sand bars on the island. The town was first settled by John Thomas and Israel Higgens in 1763 and called Eden after either the beauty of the area or after Richard Eden, an English statesman. The name was changed to Bar Harbor in 1918.

Baring: Like the nearby town of Alexander, Baring is named for Alexander Baring, Lord Ashburton, who was the British Ambassador to the United States and a landowner in Maine. First settled around 1810.

Bar Mills: Descriptive name for the bar in the river.

Barnard: First settled around 1809, the town was named for the owner of the only store, Moses Barnard.

Barred Island: Named for the sand bar that attaches it to the mainland at low tide.

Barters Island: Samuel Barter settled there in the mid 1700s.

Bartlett Island: Christopher Bartlett settled in the area in the mid 1700s.

Baskahegan: Abenaki for "branch downstream."

Basket Island: Descriptive.

Bass Harbor: Historians are not clear whether it was named after sea bass or for an early settler.

Bates Island: The Bates family was from Great Chebeague Island.

Bath: The first settlers, who came around 1640, originally called this area Long Reach. The first rights to this land were bought from an Indian sagamore (chief). When the first petition to incorporate as a town was prepared in 1781, the townspeople voted to call the town Reach, short for Long Reach. This was changed to Bath when the petition was submitted. The name comes from the famous English city of Bath, first founded by the Romans and a popular English resort at the time.

Bay Point: Descriptive name after Stage Island Bay.

Beals Island: Manwaring Beal first sailed to the island around 1773 and settled there with his family. The town was named for him. His descendants, and those of Captain John Alley, another early resident, comprise a large number of the residents today.

Bear: Many sites in Maine are named after this animal.

Beau Lake: French for "beautiful."

Beaver: Many sites in Maine are named after this animal.

Beddington: Named after Beddington, England, which is near London.

Beech: Many sites in Maine are named for beech trees.

Beehive: This small mountain on Mount Desert Island is named for its rounded shape similar to a beehive.

Belfast: An Irish settler requested that the town be named after Belfast, Ireland when the area was first settled around 1770.

Belgrade: Named after the city of the same name in Serbia. The Belgrade Lakes have the same origin.

Belmont Corner: An Americanization of the French "belle" for beautiful and "mont" for mountain.

Benedicta: Bishop Benedict Fenwick, a Catholic Bishop, bought this township in 1834 with the intention of settling a Catholic colony and starting a Catholic College. Settlers, mostly Irish, started arriving in great numbers in 1838 and though one building was finished for the college, efforts were redirected to what is now Holy Cross in Worcester, Massachusetts. The town was named after the Bishop.

Benton: Originally settled around 1775 and called Sebasticook, the name was changed in 1850 to Benton after the popular Democrat Senator from Missouri, Thomas Hart Benton.

Bernard: The mountain and town are named after Sir Francis Bernard.

Berry Mills: Jacob Berry was an early settler.

Berwick: In 1713, this area was named after Berwick, Dorsetshire, England. Settlers first came around 1624 and established many sawmills over time. It was first called Newichawannock. Berwick, from the Old English "berewic," means "barley farm."

Bethel: The town was first called Sudbury Canada because the first owners of land were from Sudbury, Massachusetts and it was on the route to Canada. The first settlers came in the late-1770s and Gould Academy was founded in 1836. Bethel means "House of God" in Hebrew and Reverend Eliphas Chapman, who came in 1789, suggested the name. Captain Twitchell proposed the name of "Ai." There is a hill in the area with a gristmill that was called Bethel Hill, and that may have been the inspiration for the name.

Biddeford: Named after Bideford, Devonshire, England. First called Saco after the river it sits on, and then Westbrook for Col. Thomas West, the name was changed in 1718 because many settlers were from the town in England. The site of the first post-Indian permanent settlement in Maine is here.

Big: Numerous lakes, ponds, streams, and other features have this descriptive word in their names. Generally, the word "big" is found in names north of an imaginary line drawn through Bangor. Places north of the line were settled later when "big" became more popular that "great," which is used frequently south of the line.

Bigelow: Major Timothy Bigelow was with Benedict Arnold on his march through Maine to Quebec during the Revolutionary War. Bigelow climbed the mountain bearing his name to scout the country ahead.

Bingham: In 1786, William Bingham bought two tracts of land totaling two million acres, one million around the Kennebec River and one million west of the Penobscot River, from General Henry Knox who had purchased the land on credit and needed money. Bingham, a wealthy banker, and later a U.S. Senator from Philadelphia, played a key role in financing the Revolutionary War. The first settler came in 1801 and the town was incorporated in 1812.

Birches: Descriptive.

Birch Harbor: Descriptive for birch trees.

Blaine: William Chandler was the first settler in 1842. First called Letter B, Range One and then Alva, the town was named Blaine when it was incorporated in 1874. It was named for James Blaine of Augusta. He was a congressman, President Harrison's Secretary of State, and the Republican nominee for president in 1884. Blaine's house in Augusta in now the Executive Mansion where the Governor lives.

Blanchard: In 1831, Charles Blanchard and Thomas Davee bought the township. Blanchard was the majority owner so the town was named after him.

Blockhouse Point: This site near Castine was once the location of a small blockhouse.

Blue Hill: First settled in 1762 by Joseph Wood and John Round. Parson Jonathan Fisher came to the area in 1796 and gave the name after climbing a hill and seeing all the surrounding hills covered with pine, fir, and spruce giving them a dark blue color. The Indians called it Awanadjo, which means "small hazy mountain."

Bog: Descriptive of the many sites with this word as part of their names.

Bolsters Mills: Isaac Bolster owned a sawmill here in 1819.

Boothbay: Named after Old Boothby in England. A legend states that the townspeople petitioned for the town to be called Townshend, but were denied because there was a town with that name in Massachusetts. The petitioner was asked about the landscape and replied that they had a harbor, "snug as a booth" and that there was a bay there too.

Bowdoin: Named for James Bowdoin, a governor of Massachusetts in 1785-86.

Bowdoinham: William Bowdoin of Boston bought this land and the town was incorporated in 1762 and named after him. Bowdoin College is named for this family.

Bowerbank: An English merchant named Bowerbank was the second owner of the land.

Boyd Lake: Named for an early settler, General J. P. Boyd.

Boyden: This lake and stream in Washington County are named for Delphia Boyden, an early settler.

Bradford: First settled in 1803, it was named for Bradford, Massachusetts, which was named for Bradford, England.

Bradley: Named for an early settler, Bradley Blackman, who came to the area about 1800.

Branch: This descriptive word is given to a number of lakes and streams.

Brandy Pond: This pond and stream were named for their brandy colored water.

Brassua: Abenaki pronunciation of "Frank," a chief's name.

Brave Boat Harbor: Named because only a "brave" boat would enter this shallow harbor.

Bremen: William Hilton was the first settler in 1735, but was driven away by Indians. He returned in 1745. The area was part of nearby Bristol, but was separated in 1828 and given its name after the German city of Bremen.

Bremen Long Island: Named for Bremen, Germany.

Brewer: Named for Colonel John Brewer, Esquire, who settled in the area in 1770.

Brewer Mountain: This mountain on Mt. Desert Island is named for Edward Brewer, a shipbuilder.

Bridgewater: This land was given by the Commonwealth of Massachusetts to Bridgewater Academy of Bridgewater, Massachusetts, and named for it when it was incorporated in 1858.

Bridgton: Moody Bridges and others were given this land in 1764 to compensate them for land they lost when the establishment of the New Hampshire/Canada line left land they owned on the Canadian side of the new line. The town was first called Pondicherry and then Bridgton to honor Moody Bridges.

Brighton: Unknown.

Brimstone Islands: Named for the black granite commonly called brimstone.

Bristol: One of the oldest settled parts of Maine, people have lived there since approximately 1625. The area was named for Bristol, England.

Broad Cove: Descriptive

Brooklin: When this area was separated from Sedgwick in 1849, the line was drawn along a brook, hence Brooklin.

Brooks: First known as Washington Plantation after the first President, the name was changed to Brooks in 1816 after Governor John Brooks of Massachusetts.

Brooksville: Named for Governor John Brooks of Massachusetts who served from 1816 to 1820. Brooks was a physician and served as an officer during the Revolutionary War.

Brookton: Originally called Jackson Brook, the name was shortened to Brookton.

Brownfield: The General Court granted land to Captain Henry Young Brown here in 1763 for his role in the French and Indian War.

Browns Head: Cyril Brown lived nearby.

Brownville: Moses Brown and Josiah Hills bought the land in this area in 1805, and the town was incorporated as Brownsville in 1824.

Brunswick: Around 1625, Thomas Purchase settled in the Brunswick area. Early names for the area include Northampton, Harwick, and Augusta. The settlers called the town Brunswick when it was incorporated in 1738. The reason is not clear, but it is likely the name was selected because the King of England at the time was of the House of Brunswick. It's also possible it was named after Brunswick, Germany, though there were no German immigrants there.

Bryant Pond: Two early settlers were named Bryant.

Bubbles: These two hills near Jordan Pond resemble breasts and early settlers called them the "boobies." Later, mapmakers changed the name to be more proper.

Buckfield: Abijah Buck moved his family here in 1777 from New Gloucester, and the town was called Buckstown until 1793. The name was changed to Buckfield when it was incorporated.

Buckmaster Neck: Several people named Buckminister lived in the area.

Bucks Harbor: Captain Thomas Buck settled in this area around 1763.

Bucksport: In 1764, Colonel Jonathan Buck settled here with his family and built a mill. In 1779, the British burned the town and the settlers fled. Colonel Buck and others returned in 1784 and rebuilt the town.

Burlington: The first settlers, including Tristam Hurd, came in 1824. It was named after Burlington, Massachusetts and was incorporated in 1832.

Burnham: Rufus Burnham, M.D., lived in nearby Unity.

Burnt: This descriptive word is given to many features in Maine. Burntcoat Harbor on Swans Island has an interesting story. When Samuel de Champlain sailed by in 1604, he called the island Brule Cote, which is French for Burnt Coast. Some

Englishman who didn't know his French corrupted it to Burnt Coat. Burnt Coat Island in Phippsburg Township is also a corruption of Brule Cote.

Bustins Island: John Bustin lived on the island in the 1600s.

The Nubble

Butter Island: Named for the butter color of the goldenrods that cover the island during the summer.

Buxton: The first minister in Buxton was the Rev. Paul Coffin, who suggested the town be named for Buxton, England, which was renowned for its medicinal springs. It has been a resort since the days of the Romans who used it as a spa.

Byron: Lieutenant John Stockbridge settled here with his family around 1815, and the town was first called Skillerton. When it was incorporated in 1833, it was named Byron after the famous poet, Lord Byron.

C

Cadillac Mountain: The King of France gave Antoine Laumet a small grant of land that included the Isle des Monts Deserts (Mount Desert Island) in 1688. Laumet, the son of a lawyer from a small town in France, had big ambitions and gave himself a name and title to match them, calling himself Antoine La Mothe, Sieur de Cadillac. Cadillac was a small town near his hometown in France. Later, he also added the title of "Seigneur des Monts Deserts" and named the highest mountain Cadillac after himself. He went on to found a small fur trading post named Detroit, today's Motor City, and later became governor of French Louisiana.

Calais: Named after Calais, France, the town lies across the St. Croix River from Dover Hill in New Brunswick, just as Calais, France lies across the English Channel from Dover in England. It was first settled in the 1760s.

Calderwood: The neck and island are named after John Calderwood who settled in the area in 1769.

Cambridge: Settled in 1804, the town is named after Cambridge, England, home of the famous University.

Camden: Called Megunticook or Macaddacut by the Indians, meaning "big mountain harbor," it was settled by James

Richards in 1769. Captain John Smith called the area Dunbarton on his map of 1614. The town was named for Charles Pratt, Lord Camden, when it was incorporated in 1791. Lord Camden was a supporter of the colonies during the Revolution.

Campbell Island: John Campbell was an early settler.

Camp Ellis: Thomas Ellis was an early settler.

Canaan: Originally called Heywoodstown, after an early settler, and then Wesserunset, the Indian name for the stream running through town, the townspeople thought both names too long at the time of incorporation in 1788. Canaan, a Biblical name, was selected because of their faith and because the area's beauty was felt to be similar to the "promised land."

Canton: Named after Canton, Massachusetts.

Cape Cottage: Descriptive.

Cape Elizabeth: Captain John Smith presented his map of New England to Prince Charles in 1615 or 1616 and asked him to give Christian names to the locations with Indian names. Charles named Cape Elizabeth for his sister, Princess Elizabeth. (He also named the area where the Pilgrims landed Plymouth, they didn't give the name, and he named Cape Ann in Massachusetts for his mother.) The first attempted settlement was in 1605 on Richmond Island, and settlements came and went on the Cape because of business opportunities and Indian hostilities throughout the 1600s.

Cape Jellison: Unknown.

Cape Neddick: Micmac Indian for "solitary." Named for the rock that stands alone there.

Cape Porpoise: Named either after the fish or Abenaki for "stopped up" with islands.

Cape Rosier: James Rosier accompanied Captain George Waymouth on a voyage to this area in 1605 and wrote a book about it called, *A True Relation of the Most Prosperous Voyage Made this Present Year, 1605, by Captain George Waymouth In the Discovery of the North Part of Virginia.* Rosier had also sailed the area with Bartholomew Gosnold in 1602.

Caratunk: Abenaki for "forbidding or crooked stream." Another source says it may also be Old Norse or Abenaki for "scraped field," because caribou would scrape the snow away with their antlers to find grass.

Cardville: The Card family were early settlers.

Caribou: First settled in 1829 by Alexander Cochrane. One of his sons shot a caribou and a nearby stream was named after the arctic animals, which, once plentiful in Maine, were rarely seen that far south at that date. The town was called Lyndon until 1877 when it was changed to Caribou. Other lakes, ponds, and streams are named for the animal.

Carmel: The Reverend Paul Ruggles was the first settler and named it for the Biblical location.

Carr: Unknown

Carrabassett: Abenaki for either, "small moose place," "sturgeon place," or "sharp rock place."

Carroll: First settled around 1830, the town is named for Daniel Carroll of Maryland who was a member of the Continental Congress and a signer of the Constitution.

Carry: Also Carrying. These features were given their names because of their history as places to carry canoes from one body of water to another.

Carthage: Named after the ancient city in North Africa.

Cary: Shepard Cary was an early lumberman in Aroostook County.

Casco: Casco may come from a longer Micmac Indian word "Aucocisco," meaning "muddy." In Abenaki, it means "great blue heron." Casco Bay may have taken this name from the muddy sections at low tide. There is another more likely source of the name. In 1525, Estaban Gomez explored the coast of Maine hoping to find riches equal to those of South America. When he sailed into Casco Bay, he thought it looked like a helmet, and "casco" is the Spanish word for helmet. He named it Bahia de Casco. It is thought by some that there are 365 islands in Casco Bay and they have been called the Calendar Islands for this reason. However, there are only 222 islands if you count rocks big enough to stand on and there are 138 good-sized islands. The town of Casco was split off from Raymond in 1841.

Castine: Baron Vincent de St. Castine lived here from 1667 to 1697. A Frenchman, he came to Canada in 1665 to command French soldiers.

Cathance: Abenaki for "principal fork."

Caucomgomac: Abenaki for "lake abounding with gulls."

Cedar: Islands, mountains, and other sites are named for cedar trees.

Centerville: Named for its central location in Washington County.

Chain: Descriptive of how lakes and ponds are linked like a chain.

Chamberlain: William Chamberlain and family were early settlers in the town in Lincoln County. The lake north of Baxter State Park is named for another family named Chamberlain who settled on the lake.

Champlain Mountain: Samuel de Champlain, the French explorer of the early 1600s, discovered Mount Desert Island among many other places. He was born in 1567 and explored the West Indies, Mexico, and Panama between 1599 and 1601. He explored Maine in 1604 and 1605 and wintered on an island in the St. Croix River. On later trips, he discovered Lake Champlain, founded a trading post where Montreal is today, and explored parts of the Great Lakes. He later was made Governor of Quebec.

Chandler: Chandler Ridge is named for Cyrus Chandler, Chandler Mountain for Mark Chandler who farmed nearby, and the rest for other settlers named Chandler.

Chandler River: Judah Chandler was an early settler near the river.

Charleston: Settled in 1795 by Joseph Bridgham, the town was called New Charleston after Charleston, Massachusetts. After Maine became a separate state in 1820, the "New" was dropped.

Charlotte: Named for the wife of an early settler.

Chase Lake: Unknown.

THE NAMES OF MAINE

Chebeague: Abenaki for "almost separated." It becomes two islands at high tide, or did when it was named.

Chelsea: Named for Chelsea, Massachusetts, which is named for the section of London with that name.

Chemo: Abenaki for "large bog."

Chemquasabamticook: Abenaki for "where there is a large lake together with a river."

Cherryfield: Located on the Narraguagus River, the town was first called by that name. The first settlers came in 1757 and the name was changed to Cherryfield when it was incorporated in 1816. The name came from cherry orchards there.

Chester: Named after Chester, New Hampshire.

Chesterville: Named after Chester, New Hampshire according to one source. Another historian says that the early settlers liked to sing and a favorite song of theirs was named "Chester." Dummer Sewall proposed naming the town after the song and it was submitted to the General Court. However, there was a Chester in Massachusetts so the General Court tacked "ville" onto the name. It was first settled in 1780.

Chesuncook: Abenaki for "at the place of the principal outlet."

China: The town was not named after the country, but for a popular hymn of the time named "China."

Chiputneticook Lakes: Abenaki for "at the place of the big hill stream."

Chisholm: Hugh Chisholm was a mill builder.

Christmas Cove: The name comes from the holiday, but it is uncertain if any of the legends can be verified, including that Norsemen spent Christmas here in 1014. Christmas Cove on Monhegan is supposed to have received that name because Captain John Smith spent Christmas here in 1614.

Churchill: The lake, and other sites with this name northwest of Baxter State Park, are named for a boy with that last name that drowned in the lake in the early 1800s.

City Point: Descriptive.

Clapboard Island: Someone thought it looked like a clapboard, or clapboards were produced here.

Clark Point: This area of Southwest Harbor is named for an early storekeeper named Nathan Clark.

Clayton: The source of the lake's name is unknown. The brook near Ashland is named for C.W. Clayton who owned a mill in the area. The brook near Washburn is named for Clair Clayton who owned a farm along the brook.

Clear: Descriptive.

Cleveland: An Acadian family Anglicized their name to this.

Cliff: Descriptive.

Clifford: Unknown.

Clifton: First called Jarvis Gore, the name Clifton is descriptive.

Clinton: Settled around 1775, the town is named for DeWitt Clinton who built the Erie Canal, was a U.S. Senator, Governor of New York, and nominee for President.

Cobbosseecontee: Abenaki for "plenty of sturgeon."

Cobscook: Malecite for "rocks under water."

Coburn Gore: The first settlers were named Coburn.

Colby: Named after Colby Buzzell.

Cold: Descriptive for the lakes, ponds, and streams with this word in their names.

Columbia: First settled in 1750 by William and Noah Mitchell, the name Columbia is derivative from Christopher Columbus and is synonymous with America. Columbia Falls has the same name with the descriptive addition for the falls located there.

Conary Island: Thomas Conary was an early settler.

Concordsville: Named after Concord, Massachusetts and the Battle of Concord.

Condon Point: John Condon settled here in the 1700s.

Connor: Named after Maine's Governor Selden Connor who fought in the Civil War, becoming a Brigadier General of Volunteers.

Convene: Originally called New Limington, there was already another post office with that name. Ladies discussing this thought it would be convenient to have a post office in their town and one lady suggested they call it Convene.

Cooks Corner: Stephan Cook settled here in 1764.

Coombs: The hill and neck are named for Anthony Coombs who settled in the area before 1775. The island is named for Joseph Coombs who lived here around 1774.

Cooper: Settled around 1812, the town is named for General John Cooper, a leading citizen.

Coopers Mills: Leonard Cooper settled here around 1833.

Corea: Named after the country of Korea.

Chickadee, the Maine State Bird

Corinna: Dr. John Warren, the brother of General Joseph Warren who died during the Battle of Bunker Hill, bought this land from Massachusetts in 1804 and the town is named after his daughter. The settlers originally petitioned for it to be called North Wood.

Corinth: First settled in 1792, the town takes its name from the ancient city in Greece.

Cornish: Cornish pertains to Cornwall, England, and it is thought that Francis Small, an early settler, came from there.

Cornville: First called Bernardstown after Moses Bernard, one of the first owners of the land, the name was changed to

Cornville, because of the excellent farmland, when the town was incorporated in 1798.

Costigan: Three brothers named Costigan settled here.

Cousins: The river and island in Cumberland County are named for John Cousins who bought the land in 1645. He was born in England in 1596 and came to Falmouth in 1631. The Indians called the island Susquesong.

Cow: The island is named for the cows that grazed here.

Crabtree Point: Agreen Crabtree was an early settler.

Cranberry Isles: Named for a cranberry bog on the largest island.

Crawford: William Crawford was a U.S. Senator from Georgia, Minister to France, Secretary of War, and Secretary of the Treasury from 1816 to 1825.

Crescent Beach: This descriptive name has been given to many beaches.

Crescent Lake: Descriptive.

Criehaven: This area of Ragged Island was named for Robert Crie, who owned this area in the mid 1800s. He put shipwrecked sailors up in his home.

Crockett Cove: Josiah Crockett was an early settler.

Crooked: The names of the lake and brooks with this moniker are descriptive.

Cross: Descriptive of having to cross something to get from one point to another.

Crotch Island: Descriptive of its shape. Granite is still quarried here.

Crouseville: Gould Crouse was an early settler.

Crow: Many places have this descriptive name.

Crowley Island: Green Crowley was a sea captain.

Crystal: Crystal Stream, which flows through town, flows from Crystal Lake, named for its crystal clear water.

Cuckolds: A cuckold is the husband of an unfaithful wife and the men that have been wrecked on these rocks thought it an appropriate name.

Cumberland: The Duke of Cumberland was the son of King George II. John Philips was the first settler sometime shortly before 1640. Cumberland County was created in 1760.

Cundys Harbor: The harbor and nearby points are named for William Cundy, who lived in the area in the early 1700s.

Cunliffe: The many features with this name honor a well-known river driver named Will Cunliffe.

Cupissic: Abenaki for "impassable branch."

Cupsuptic: Abenaki for "a closed up stream."

Curtis Corner: William Curtis was an early settler.

Cushing: First called St. George, the first settlers came in 1733. The name was changed to Cushing in 1803 after Thomas Cushing who was Lt. Governor of Massachusetts from 1783 to 1788.

Cushing Island: Colonel Ezekiel Cushing settled on the island in the 1760s. It was first called Portland Island and then Bangs Island, after Joshua Bangs, until it was sold to a distant relative of Ezekiel Cushing who was named Lemuel Cushing, and the name went back to Cushing.

Cut: Named for a canal that was cut from Cut Lake to Hay Brook to drive logs to market in Bangor.

Cutler: Joseph Cutler was an early landowner from Newburyport, Massachusetts.

Cutts: Many features in York County are named for Richard, John, and Robert Cutts, who came from Wales in the 1600s.

Cuxabexis: Malecite for "little, swift water."

D

Daigle: Early settlers were named Daigle.

Dallas: Possibly for Vice President George M. Dallas who served from 1845-49.

Damariscotta: The origin of this name is not clear. Some think it is from the Abenaki "Madamescontee" for "place of abundance of fishes" or "abundance of alewives" (a type of fish). Others think it is not an Indian word at all, but may be a made-up name, combining the names of Humphrey Damarell and John Cotta, early residents. The first settlers came around 1640, though permanent settlers didn't come until after 1745.

Damariscove Island: Humphrey Damarell operated a busy trading post on the island for almost 40 years beginning in 1608. It was called Damarell's Cove and was shortened to its current form over time. The Nature Conservancy owns the island today and there are no residents, but this island was important in the early commerce of Maine.

Danforth: Thomas Danforth was granted the first half township here.

Danville: Uncertain, but possibly for Danville, Vermont.

Dark Harbor: Dark, in the nautical language of the 1800s, meant something was hard to see.

Davis: There are many places with this name in Penobscot County. The hill and brook near Charleston are for a family with that name that settled here. The pond near Eddington was named for Captain Samuel Davis who settled here around 1800. The hill near Newburgh is named for Willard Davis who had a farm nearby. Other sites are named for a trapper named Davis. In Piscataquis County, most of the features with this name honor General A. Davis who was an early proprietor. Davis Beach in Washington County is named for a settler with that name that lived here in the 1880s.

Days Ferry: The Day family ran a ferry at this site.

Days Mills: C. Day was an early settler.

Deadman Cove: This cove on Monhegan Island was named for two bodies found there.

Deblois: Originally called Anneburg after the first landowner's daughter, the name was changed to Deblois when it was incorporated in 1850. Thomas Deblois was president of the City Bank of Portland, which was involved in the financing of the land. He served in the Legislature and was a U.S. Attorney.

Deboullie: Named for a lumberman with that name.

Debsconeag: Abenaki for "ponds at the waterway."

Dedham: First settled around 1810, the town was named for Dedham, Massachusetts.

Deering: Named for Nathaniel and John Deering.

Deer Isle: Descriptive. The first settlers came in the 1760s.

Denmark: Named after the country, though one story says it was named after Danish seamen who fought courageously against English warships. Daniel Boston settled here in 1775.

Dennysville: Monsiuer Nicholas Denys, a Frenchman and lieutenant governor of Acadia, lived in this area in the early 1600s. An Indian chief in the late 1700s was named Denny and Denny's River, which goes through town, was named after the chief whose name came from the Frenchman. The town took its name from the river. The first settlers came from Hingham, Massachusetts in 1786.

Depot: The lake, stream and mountain were named for a supply camp that was in the area.

Derby: Originally called Medford Junction, the name was changed by the president of the Bangor and Aroostook Railroad when the railroad's shops were moved here. Derby is of English origin.

Desolation: The brook and pond were given this descriptive name for their location in the middle of nowhere.

Detroit: Detroit is the French word for "straights" in a river. The town was first called Chandlerville and named after the straights of the Sebasticook River in 1848.

Devils Island: Named for the famous prison island in French Guiana. Prisoners worked at the quarry on the island.

Dexter: Named for Samuel Dexter who ran for governor of Massachusetts in 1816 and lost. First settled around 1800.

Dickey: William Dickey was an early settler.

Dixfield: Dr. Elijah Dix of Boston owned the land in the area around 1800.

Dixmont: Dr. Elijah Dix owned the land in this area. He gave the town a library in return for the town being named after him.

Dole: The source of the name for these features in Somerset County is unknown.

Dorr Mountain: George Dorr gave this mountain to be part of Acadia National Park. Dorr was instrumental in the formation of the park, convincing many other landowners to donate land.

Douglas Hill: John and Andrew Douglas settled here in the late 1820s.

Dover-Foxcroft: Charles Vaughn and John Merrick bought this land around 1800 and the town was named after Dover, England where the Vaughn family originated. Joseph Foxcroft bought this land from Bowdoin College in 1800. Foxcroft gave land for schools and books for the town library in appreciation of the town naming itself after him. In 1922, the towns were combined.

Down East: This term is often used as a nickname for Maine. However, Mainers consider down east to be the coastline east of approximately Mt. Desert Island. The term comes from sailing jargon as the prevailing winds in Maine in the summer come from the Southwest. A boat sailing east was sailing downwind, hence the term down east.

Drakes Island and Beach: Robert Drake, who fought in the Revolutionary War, owned the island.

Dresden Mills: First settled in 1752, the town was named after Dresden, Germany, where some of the early settlers originated.

Drisko Island: Joseph Drisko and his family settled here in the late 1700s.

Dryden: John Dryden was a director of the Farmington Insurance Company in the 1850s.

Dry Mills: Descriptive.

Duck: Many sites in Maine are named after this waterfowl.

Ducktrap: The Indians trapped ducks in this area while they were molting and could not fly away.

Dunham Point: Elijah Dunham lived here.

Durham: First settled around 1770, the town was named for Durham, England, the hometown of one of the landowners.

Dyer Neck: The neck and other features are named for Henry Dyer who lived here in the mid 1700s.

Dyer Point: This point and cove on Cape Elizabeth is named for the Dyer brothers who lived there in the early 1800s.

E

Eagle: In 1839, Major Hastings Strickland named Eagle Lake for the bald eagles in the area. Other sites are also named for this majestic bird. Admiral Peary, the first man to reach the North Pole, had his home on Eagle Island in Casco Bay. It is a state park today.

Eastbrook: The drainage of part of the town flows into the east branch of the Union River. First settled around 1800.

Eastern Mark Island: The island near Stonington marks the end of the Deer Island Thorofare.

Easton: Its location on the eastern edge of Maine and Aroostook County gives Easton its name. This area remained under Massachusetts' ownership after Maine statehood, until Maine bought all the land still owned by Massachusetts around 1854. The first settlers came around 1855.

Eastport: First called Moose Island, the name was changed to Eastport for its eastern location when the town was incorporated in 1798.

Ebeemee: Not certain, but may be Abenaki for "extended" or "berries."

Echo: Descriptive

Eddington: Colonel Jonathan Eddy and his soldiers were given 9,000 acres of land for their service in the Revolutionary War. They first settled here in 1787.

Eaton: Henry Eaton was president of the Eaton Lumber Company.

Edgecomb: Lord Mount Edgecomb, a friend of the colonies during the Revolutionary War, is honored with this name. His ancestor, Sir Richard Edgecomb, was first granted this land around 1637, but the grant was found to be invalid.

Egg Rocks: These small islands in Muscongus Bay gained their names because Indians gathered bird eggs for food on them.

Eggemoggin Reach: Malecite for "fish weir place."

Eliot: Robert Eliot was a 1701 graduate of Harvard, a member of the Provincial Council of New Hampshire, and lived in Kittery. The first settler appears to be Nicholas Frost around 1636.

Eliot Mountain: Charles William Eliot, a former president of Harvard, was instrumental in establishing Acadia National Park in the early 1900s.

Ellingwood Rock: John Wallace Ellingwood was an early settler.

Ellis: The town is named for the Ellis family and the pond for a different Ellis family.

Ellsworth: First called Union River and then Bowdoin, the townspeople asked for the name Sumner, but another town in Maine already had that name. The General Court of

Massachusetts gave it the name of Ellsworth after Oliver Ellsworth, who was a Massachusetts delegate to the Constitutional Convention of 1787. It was incorporated in 1800.

Embdem: A town in Germany.

Emery Mills: Simon Emery owned the sawmill in town before 1775.

Endless Lake: Descriptive of a long lake.

Enfield: Named after Enfield, England.

Englishman Bay: An Englishman named Day settled on the shore of this bay.

Eskutassis: Abenaki for "small trout."

Estcourt Station: The northernmost town in Maine. It is named after Estcourt, Canada.

Etna: First called Crosbytown after the landowner in 1807, which is when the first settlers came, until 1820, when the name Etna was selected after Mt. Etna in Sicily.

Eustis: Charles Eustis and a man named Clark bought this land around 1831. First called Hanover and then Jackson, Eustis was selected in 1857 in honor of the previous landowner.

Exeter: First named Blaisdelltown after an early landowner, the first settlers came around 1801. When the town was incorporated in 1811, the name Exeter was selected to honor Exeter, New Hampshire where some of the early settlers had previously lived.

F

Fairbanks: Colonel Joseph Fairbanks owned a mill here in 1792.

Fairfield: Settled in 1774, the towns name is descriptive for the beauty of the area.

Fairmount: Descriptive.

Falls: Descriptive.

Falmouth: Falmouth, England sits at the mouth of the Fal River, and Falmouth, Maine was named after that English town. Arthur Macksworth first settled in the area around 1632. The town originally included the greater Portland area.

Farmingdale: The first settlers came in 1787 and the town's name is descriptive for the excellent farmland in the valley (dale).

Farmington: The name is descriptive of the good farmland. Local Indians grew corn here before the area was settled by Europeans. The area was first explored in 1776 and the first settlers came around 1780.

Fayette: The name honors the Marquis de Lafayette, the French soldier who was of tremendous help to the colonies during the Revolutionary War. The first settlers came around 1779.

Ferry Beach: There was a ferry landing here.

Fish: The lake and river in Aroostook County are named for Ira Fish, who was in the area in the early 1800s. Other sites with this name are descriptive.

Fishermans Island: Descriptive.

Five Islands: Descriptive.

Flag Island: Named for a type of flower that grows here.

Flagstaff: Benedict Arnold had a flag on a flagstaff in his camp in this area in northwest Maine on his march to Quebec during the Revolutionary War. Flagstaff Mountain in Washington County is named for flagstaffs that surveyors used to hold flags so they could be seen from a distance.

Flint Island: The Indians got flint for weapons on this island.

Flye: The point and island are named for James Flye, who settled in the area in the late 1700s.

Flying Mountain: An Indian legend claims that a part of another mountain flew off and created this mountain on Mount Desert Island.

Flying Point: Named for the waterfowl that flew over from one bay to the next.

Fogg Point: Someone named Fogg lived here in the 1800s.

Fore River: Descriptive of its location.

Forest City: Descriptive.

Fort Fairfield: John Fairfield was Governor of Maine from 1839 to 1843 when a fort was built at this location during the border disputes and named for him. The first settlers came in the late 1820s. The land was originally granted by the General Court of Massachusetts to the town of Plymouth, Massachusetts to help them pay for a breakwater in 1806.

Fort Gorges: This run down stone fort in Casco Bay is the only site in Maine named for the Father of Maine, Sir Ferdinando Gorges.

Fort Kent: The first settlers were French Acadians, who came around 1829. A fort was built in 1841 and named after Governor Edward Kent. Many soldiers stayed in the area after the border disputes were settled.

Fortunes Rocks: Named for luck.

Fosters Corner: The Foster family were early settlers.

Fox Islands Thorofare: In 1603, the explorer Martin Pring sailed between two islands where he saw many foxes and named the islands the Fox Islands. The passage between them became the Fox Island Thorofare. The islands have since been named Vinalhaven and North Haven.

Frankfort: Named after Frankfort, Germany, the first settlers came around 1770.

Franklin: Benjamin Franklin is honored by this town's name. Franklin County was created in 1838 and also honors Ben Franklin.

Freedom: Named in 1813 when the spirit of patriotism ran high due to the War of 1812, the townspeople selected this name to reflect their patriotic feelings.

Freeport: This area was originally part of what the Indians called Westcustago and then became part of North Yarmouth. When the town petitioned to become a separate incorporated entity, they asked to be called Greene. Another town in Maine had already been given that name and the General Court chose Freeport instead. It is not certain why, but there are two theories as to the name. The first and most likely is that the name describes the openness of the harbor or just recognizes the fact that it is a port. The second is that it is named after Sir Andrew Freeport, a character in a novel by Joseph Addison. The first settlers came around 1750 and called the town Harraseeket or Harrisicket, which is the Indian name for the stream that runs through the town.

Freese Island: George Freese was an early settler.

Frenchboro: The origin is unknown though the French first inhabited this entire area.

French Island: Unknown, though there were families of this name in the area.

Frenchman Bay: Named for the French ships that gathered here to fight the British.

Frenchville: First called Dickeysville, the name was changed because many of the residents were of French nationality.

Friendship: Originally called Medumcook, its Indian name meaning "sandy harbor" was a misnomer, as the harbor is a rocky one. The name was changed to Friendship in 1807 because of the friendliness of the people. The first settlers came around 1750.

Friendship Long Island: Named for the town.

Frye: Named for a family of that name.

Fryeburg: Captain Joseph Frye of Andover, Massachusetts was granted this land in 1762 for his service in the French and Indian War. When they surveyed the state line some of his grant ended up being in New Hampshire. He lost that land, but was given more in Lovell as recompense. The Indians called the area Pegwacket or Pequawket. The first settlers came around 1763. It was the first town settled in the White Mountain region of New Hampshire and Maine.

G

Gardiner: Dr. Sylvester Gardiner was one of the early landowners, possessing 1,200 acres by 1770. He owned the first drug store in Boston in the mid 1700s and became wealthy from it.

Gardner Lake: Named for Laban Gardner who settled in the area in the 1780s.

Garland: Originally granted to Williams College in 1796, the college sold the land to a group of investors including Levi Lincoln and the area was called Lincolnville. Joseph Garland was the first settler in 1802 and the townspeople met in his house in 1811 to decide to petition for incorporation and voted to name the town after him.

Gassabias: Abenaki for "small, clear water lake."

Gay Island: Lozen Gay settled here in 1789.

Georgetown: First colonized in 1607 and permanently settled around 1625, the area was called Parker's Island after an early settler. The name was changed to Georgetown in 1741 to honor King George I of England.

Gerrish Island: Timothy Gerrish bought this island in 1709.

Gilbertville: An early family of settlers was named Gilbert.

Gilead: First settled around 1780, the town is named for the Balm of Gilead trees that grew here.

Glenburn: Originally called Dutton after an early landowner, the name was changed to a Scottish word meaning "narrow valley" (glen) and, "small stream" (burn).

Glen Cove: Descriptive, glen meaning narrow valley in Scottish.

Golden Ridge: Descriptive of the beautiful, productive farmland.

Gooch's Beach: John Gooch settled here in the 1660s.

Goodwins Mills: In 1787, Nathaniel Goodwin built the first mill on this site.

Googins Island: Named for the family that settled here in 1763.

Goose: Many sites are named for geese. The small islands off Lower Goose Island in Casco Bay are called The Goslings.

Gooseberry: Descriptive name for the gooseberries found here.

Gorham: First settled in 1736, the town was called Narragansett Number 7 because it was granted to a group of men for their service in the Narragansett War of 1675. The area was later called Gorhamtown after Captain John Gorham, who was one of the men granted the land. The name was shortened to Gorham in 1764. Captain John Phinney and his son cut down the first tree here in 1736.

Gott: These islands are named after Daniel Gott, who owned them in the late 1700s.

Gouldsboro: Named after Robert Gould, one of the early landowners who bought it in 1764.

Graham Lake: Named for Edward Graham Sr., who worked for Bangor Hydro-Electric Co.

Grand: Descriptive of many sites.

Grand Isle: Named by early French Acadian settlers after a large island in the St. John River.

Gray: First settled in 1750, the town is named for Thomas Gray of Boston, an early landowner.

Great Diamond Island: First called Hog Island, someone changed the name to this more appealing moniker.

Great Pond: Descriptive.

Great Wass Island: Wilmot Wass settled on the island in the mid 1700s.

Greeley Landing: Eden Greeley was an early settler around 1822.

Green Island: Descriptive. The island near Vinalhaven is named for Joseph Green, who escaped from Indians after they killed his family in the mid 1700s.

Greenbush: The name is descriptive for the forest. The first settlers came around 1820.

Greene: First called Littleborough after Moses Little, an early landowner who had come from Newbury, Massachusetts. The name was changed to Greene in 1788 to honor General Nathaniel Greene, a great figure of the Revolutionary War. The town was settled in the 1770s. In their original petition for incorporation, they asked to be called Greenland.

Greenfield: The name is either descriptive for the green fields or from Greenfield, Massachusetts.

Green Lake: Descriptive.

Greenlaw Neck: The neck and cove are named for William Greenlaw, who lived in the area in the mid 1700s.

Greenville: The name is descriptive of the green forests. The area was settled in the 1820s.

Greenwood: Though the name may be descriptive, the town is probably named for Alexander Greenwood, who surveyed the area.

George Head Islands: The George family lived in the area.

Grindstone: Boatmen used to sharpen their axes at this site.

Grindstone Neck: A ship loaded with grindstones wrecked on this neck.

Grove: Descriptive for a grove of trees.

Guerette: Named after a family of settlers.

Guilford: Named after Guildford, England.

H

Hadley: The lakes and brook are named for several families with that name.

Hafey: Unknown.

Haines Landing: Unknown.

Hale: A man named Hale ran the Post Office in nearby Mexico and the town is named after him.

Hallowell: Benjamin Hallowell of Boston was an early landowner. The first settler, Deacon Pease Clark, came in 1762.

Hamlin: The name honors Hannibal Hamlin, who was Vice President of the United States.

Hampden: First settled in 1767 and called Wheelersburg after the first settler, the town was renamed in 1794 for John Hampden, a patriot of England in the 1600s, who protested against being forced to lend money to the King of England.

Hancock: John Hancock, a successful Boston merchant, was a key leader of the rebels seeking independence from England. He was governor of Massachusetts from 1780 to 1785 and again from 1787 to 1793. The Massachusetts's State House sits on land that was Hancock's pasture and his house was just next to it. The town was settled in 1764. The County is named after him and he was governor when the County was created.

Hanover: King George III of England's family name is Hanover as his ancestors came from the Hanover province of Germany.

Harbor: Descriptive.

Harborside: Descriptive.

Harfords Point: William Harford and William Churchill camped here sometime before 1800. Their campfire got out of control and burned much of the area.

Harmony: First settled in 1796, the town was called Vaughnstown after Charles Vaughn an early landowner. The town was renamed Harmony in 1804, for the spirit of harmony that existed between the settlers.

Harpswell: This peninsula was originally part of North Yarmouth, and was likely named after Harpswell, England. It later became part of Brunswick and was incorporated as a town in 1758.

Harraseeket: Possibly Abenaki for "full of obstacles." It may have been a local Indian's name.

Harrington: This name was first given by a surveyor in the early 1600s to the present area of Bristol and was named after an English nobleman and writer. After the name was changed to Bristol, the name was used for several months by the present town of Augusta and was then selected by the settlers of the present Harrington. The namesake of Lake Harrington near Baxter State Park is unknown.

The Gazebo

Harrison: Harrison Gray Otis of Boston, an early landowner in this area, was a real estate developer who developed much of Beacon Hill. He became Mayor of Boston and was a U.S. Senator. He had three houses built on Beacon Hill in Boston that were designed by Charles Bulfinch who designed the Massachusetts State House. Several of these houses are open to the public today. John and Nathan Carsley were the first settlers in the area in 1792.

Harrow: Unknown.

Hartford: Edmund Irish first settled the area in 1788 and the town is named after Hartford, Connecticut, which is named for Hartford, England.

Hartland: Hart is an old English name for "deer," and the name means "the land of the deer." Some say it means "the heart of the hills." Stephen Hartwell built the first house there about 1800, but it doesn't appear that the town is named after him.

Haskell Island: Captain Haskell was the skipper of a sailing vessel.

Hastings: A man named Hastings had a mill at this site.

Hatchet Cove: Legend says the Indians buried a hatchet here as a gesture of peace.

Hay: Descriptive of the hay found or used near the many sites with this word in their names.

Haymock: The Abenaki name for this lake and mountain is "pongokwahemook," which means "woodpecker place." Haymock is taken from the last part of the Indian name.

Haynesville: Originally called Forkstown, due to its proximity to the fork of the Mattawamkeag River, the name was changed to honor Alvin Haynes, an early settler around 1835.

Head Harbor Island: Descriptive of its location at the head of Moosabec Reach and Chandler Bay.

Head Tide: Descriptive.

Hebron: The land in this area was granted to Alexander Shepard of Newton, Massachusetts in 1777 on the condition that he deliver a map of Maine and settle ten families in the area in ten years. The town had several names until the settlers asked for the name Columbia at incorporation in 1792. The General Court denied the request and gave the name Hebron after the Biblical city in Israel.

Hermon: Means "sacred" or "forbidden" in Hebrew. Mt. Hermon in Israel may have been the site of the transfiguration of Jesus. It was first settled around 1784.

Heron: Descriptive for the long-legged bird.

Hersey: First settled in 1839, the town is named for General Samuel Hersey, an early landowner.

Hewett Island: Captain Soloman Hewett lived here.

Higgins Beach: The Higgins family lived here.

Highland Lake: Descriptive. The town was first named Duck Pond and the settlers considered the present name to be more desirable. Highland Lake in Bridgton was originally called Crotched Pond, but the residents wanted a nicer name.

Highpine: Descriptive.

Hills Beach: Major Roger Hill settled in the area in the 1660s.

Hinckley: Originally called East Fairfield, the U.S. Post Office asked that the name be changed because there are so many towns of that name in the country. G.W. Hinckley ran a school and home for boys and girls here, and received more mail than anyone else, so they named the town after him.

Hiram: The name honors Biblical King Hiram of Tyre.

Hockomock Point: An Abenaki name that may mean "place of walls of sharp logs driven into ground."

Hodgdon: John Hodgdon of Ware, New Hampshire, and Nathaniel Ingersoll of New Gloucester, bought the land for $5,760 in 1802. The first settler came around 1824.

Holden: Named after Holden, Massachusetts, which was named for Samuel Holden, a London merchant who aided the colonies.

Holeb: This pond, falls, stream and other sites are named for Holeb Nichols, who trapped in the area.

Hollis Center: First called Phillipsburg in 1798, it was changed in 1811 because the townspeople considered Phillipsburg too long to spell and too hard to pronounce. Hollis was the family name of the Duke of Newcastle who supported the colonists. Some say it is named for Hollis, New Hampshire.

Hope: There are two versions of how the town was named. The first says that the settlers felt it was a land of hope. The second is that when the town was surveyed, the corner posts had the letters E H P O on them and when they were discussing what to call the town someone said the survey post letters could be arranged to spell HOPE. Hope Island in Casco Bay is named for a family of that name that lived on the island.

Hot Brook Lake: The lake and streams are not called hot because of hot springs that would make the water hot, but because the brooks rarely froze.

Houghton: Unknown.

Houlton: The Joseph Houlton family moved here with the Putnam family from Salem, Massachusetts around 1805.

House Island: Christopher Leavitt and ten men built a stone house on this island in 1623. Leavitt was the first settler here after being granted 6,000 acres for serving as the King's forester.

Howes Corner: Dr. Timothy Howe settled here around 1804.

Howland: John Howland was on the Mayflower. He signed the Mayflower Compact and was an agent at the Augusta post of the Plymouth Company. The town wanted to honor one of the Pilgrim Fathers.

Hoyt Neck: Named for settlers of that name in the 1770s.

Hudson: First settled in 1800, the town was called Jackson

Plantation after Andrew Jackson, then Kirkland, and finally Hudson, after Hudson, Massachusetts.

Hulls Cove: Captain Samuel Hull settled here sometime before 1796.

Hunnewell: The point and beach are named for Ambrose Hunniwell, a settler in the early 1700s.

Hurd: The corner near Dover-Foxcroft is named for E.G. Hurd, who lived in the area in the 1880s. Several of the ponds may have been named for Josiah Hurd, who farmed in the county. The others are unknown.

Hurricane: The island and other features near Vinalhaven were named for hurricanes that hit in the area. Legend says that one hurricane hit the same day William Vinal bought Hurricane Island. The island was a significant quarry. Today, it is home to an Outward Bound program.

Hypocrites: Nearby Fisherman's Island was called "Epituse" by the Abenakis, meaning "it lies in the water." This name was Anglicized to Hippocras and then to Hypocrites and the name was transferred to the rocks near Fisherman's Island.

I

Indian: These descriptive names honor local Indians.

Ironbound Island: The name describes its rocky condition.

Island Falls: Descriptive for the island in the middle of the falls. First settled in 1842.

Isle au Haut: Named "Ille Haulte" by Samuel de Champlain, the name means "high island" in French. It became semi-Anglicized to today's name over time. It was first settled in 1792. Isle au Haut Mountain on Vinalhaven is so named because you can see Isle au Haut from it.

Isles of Shoals: Captain John Smith of Jamestown fame sailed by these islands in 1614 and gave his name to them. That didn't last long as fishermen began calling them Isles of Shoals, for the shallow water found around them. Fishermen used the islands from the early 1600s, and there were two taverns by 1628. The population grew to around 600 families by the 1770s. All families were ordered to move to the mainland during the Revolution and the islands remained empty until 1820 when people began to move back. The first island hotel in Maine was built on Appledore Island in 1848 and other hotels followed, making the islands a popular destination for vacationers in the second half of the 1800s. Today, the islands house a religious retreat and a marine research laboratory operated by the University of New Hampshire and Cornell University.

Islesboro: Descriptive for being a town on an island. First settled in 1760.

J

Jackman: The Jackman family were the first settlers.

Jackson: The name honors Revolutionary War General Henry Jackson, who was an early landowner. It was first settled around 1798.

Jacksonville: Named for President Andrew Jackson who was supported by the early settlers.

Jacquish Island: Lt. Richard Jaques was an early settler and Indian fighter.

Jay: The town was first called Phipps-Canada for David Phipps, who was given land for his service in the French War of 1755. When it was incorporated in 1795, it was named for John Jay, who was the first Chief Justice of the United States Supreme Court, served as ambassador to Spain and France, and was governor of New York. The area is famous for its white granite, which as been used to build the Marshall Field Store in Chicago, the Princeton College Chapel, the Hibernia Bank in San Francisco, and many other buildings.

Jefferson: First settled just before the Revolutionary War, the town was incorporated in 1807 when Thomas Jefferson was president, and was named to honor him. The land was originally granted to William Bradford of Mayflower fame in 1630.

Jemtland: Named by the first Swedish settlers for their home province of Jamtland.

Jewell Island: George Jewell bought the island in 1637.

Job Island: Named for Job Pendleton.

Johns River: The name of Sir John Towne is placed near the river and bay in Bristol Township on a 1614 map. It may be named for Captain John Smith who explored and mapped this area in 1614.

Jo-Mary: These sites honor an Indian chief of that name.

Jones Pond: Unknown.

Jonesboro: John Coffin Jones and others were granted this land in 1789. The area was originally called Chandler's River after the first settler who came around 1763.

Jonesport: First settled in 1772 by Francis Cummings, the town, like nearby Jonesboro, is named after John Coffin Jones, who was given 48,160 acres in 1789 as compensation for a sloop he lost during the British siege of Castine.

Jordan Island: This island in Frenchman Bay was named for H.W. Jordan who lived here in the 1880s.

Jordan Pond: The pond and ridge are named for George and J.S. Jordan. These brothers had a lumber camp on the pond.

Junior: The origin of the name for this lake, stream, and mountain are unknown.

K

Katahdin: Abenaki for "great mountain." Rising to 5,268 feet, it is the tallest mountain in Maine. Mt. Katahdin is the northern terminus of the Appalachian Trail.

Keegan: Named after Peter Keegan.

Kenduskeag: Abenaki for "eel place" or "eel weir place." Samuel de Champlain saw Indians trapping eels around Bangor when he went up the Penobscot in 1604. The name originally included the area around Bangor too.

Kennebago Lake: Abenaki for "long pond" or "large lake."

Kennebec: Abenaki for "long reach" or "long level water." It describes the part of the river below Augusta. The County was established in 1799.

Kennebunk: Abenaki for "long sandbar" and in Micmac it means "long cut bank," referring to the view of the river from the sea. The first settlement was in 1643, though the first permanent settler didn't come until 1718.

Kennebunkport: The name is descriptive for the port area of Kennebunk. It was first called Cape Porpoise in 1653, but the first settlers left due to Indian troubles. Settlers returned in 1718 and called the town Arundel, after the Earl of Arundel. In 1821, the name was changed to the present one.

Kents Hill: Captain Warren Kent and Charles Kent were the first settlers sometime before 1793.

Kezar Falls: George Kezar was a well-known trapper and hunter in the area in the 1780s.

Kimball Island: Solomon Kimball lived here around 1775.

Kineo: Indian legend says that wicked Chief Kineo was exiled by his tribe and lived on Mt. Kineo. Another legend says that Glooskap, an Indian spirit, killed a moose and it became Mt. Kineo. In Abenaki, Kineo means "sharp peak" or "sharp rock."

Kingfield: William King was the first governor of Maine when it became a state in 1820. He was an early landowner and later acquired several mills around the area and built a large mansion there.

Kingman: In the 1870s, the firm of Shaw and Kingman built a leather tannery here. The town was named after R.S. Kingman when it was incorporated in 1873.

Kingsbury: Judge Sanford Kingsbury bought a large parcel of land here in 1833 and the first settlers came in 1834. Judge Kingsbury moved here in 1835 and lived here until his death.

Kinney Shores: Aaron McKinney owned land here in the 1730s.

Kittery: The town is named for Kittery Court, a manor in Kingsweare, Devon, England. The Shapleigh family, the first settlers and landowners of Kittery, came from Kingsweare and Kittery is the oldest town in Maine. It was first settled in the 1620s and was incorporated in 1647.

Knowles Corner: Henry Knowles settled here in 1843.

Knox: General Henry Knox was a good friend of George Washington. He commanded the artillery of the Continental Army during the Revolutionary War and was Secretary of War from 1785 to 1794. Knox led the group that brought the captured cannons from Fort Ticonderoga to Boston, which were vital in forcing the British to leave Boston in 1776. After the War, the General Court of Massachusetts was desperate to raise money to pay off Revolutionary War debts and decided to sell land in the District of Maine. Sales did not go well at first until Knox, ever the speculator, with some partners bought two million acres. One million were along the Kennebec and one million were in 52 townships west of the Penobscot. The transaction was valued between $400,000 and $500,000, but they only put down $10,000. Looking for additional money, he called on his friend William Bingham, a wealthy banker from Philadelphia. Bingham bought the land from Knox. Knox married Samuel Waldo's granddaughter, inheriting Waldo's vast land holdings. They lived in a magnificent mansion in Thomaston called Montpelier, where they enjoyed the life of a nobleman and his wife, entertaining prestigious visitors. Knox was involved in many businesses, including making lime, lumber mills, agriculture, and land development. Knox County, formed from portions of Waldo and Lincoln Counties in 1860, was the last county to be created in Maine.

Kokadjo: Abenaki for "kettle mountain." Indian legend says that Glooskap, a demon, killed a moose that became Mt. Kineo. When he chased the moose's calf, he threw his kettle away so he wouldn't be burdened, and it became a mountain.

L

Lagrange: This town was known as Down East, Oxford and Hammond until it was incorporated under the name Lagrange, which was the name of Lafayette's estate.

Lake Moxie: Moxie is said to be Indian for "dark water."

Lake Parlin: Unknown.

Lake View: Descriptive.

Lakewood: Descriptive.

Lambert Lake: Settled in 1754 by Sheribiah and Robert Lambert.

Lamoine: Captain Isaac Gilpatric first settled the area in 1774. Several French settlers came soon after and one was named De LaMoine. This is the area where several Jesuits briefly had a Mission in 1613. They were defeated by the British Admiral Samuel Argall, who set 15 of the French adrift in a small boat, and took the rest with him back to Jamestown and then to England.

Langley: Unknown.

Larone: At a meeting to choose a name for the settlement, a question was asked about how the mail would get there and another question was asked about what to call the town. A man named Emery owned a roan horse called The Roan. In answer to the first question, he replied, "The Roan." The person asking the second question said, "What kind of name is that?" Emery, seeing the confusion, said that by changing "the" to "La" and adding it to roan they would have a good name. Probably just a story, but no other explanation is known.

Lasell Island: Ellison Laselle was the first settler.

Lawry: The Lawry family dates back to 1754, and the town was named in the 1900s for their descendants.

Lazygut Island: One definition of "gut" is a narrow passage of water. There is a narrow passage between Deer Isle and Little Lazygut Island and another between it and Lazygut Island. They are easy—or lazy—to navigate.

Lebanon: First settled in the 1730s and 40s, the area went without a name until it was incorporated in 1767. It was named after the Middle Eastern country and was the first town in Maine to be given a name from the Bible.

Lee: This area was originally granted to Williams College in 1805, which sold part of it to Nathaniel Ingersoll, who began clearing land in 1823. Jeremiah Fifield and his wife were the first settlers. They were given 100 acres because she was the first woman to settle in the area. The town is probably named for Stephan Lee, an early settler, though it may have been named for General Lee of Revolutionary War fame. An author of a history of Lee says there is a legend that the townspeople couldn't agree on a name and decided to name the town after the next baby born, which happened to be a Lee.

Leeds: First settled by Thomas and Roger Stinchfield in 1779, who trapped in the area and who had fought in the French and Indian War. Their father was born in Leeds, England and the town was named in honor of that town.

Levant: Levant means "orient" or "east" and specifically describes the Eastern Mediterranean. The first settler was Joseph Clark, who came from Nova Scotia around 1789. The name probably comes from the Levant Plateau area of Nova Scotia.

Lewiston: The area including present day Lewiston was first granted in 1632 and had a series of different owners until 1768, when the owners granted the land around Lewiston to Jonathan Bagley and Moses Little with the provision that the town be called Lewiston. Legend says that a drunken Indian named Lewis fell in the falls and drowned and the falls were named after him and the town after the falls. Paul Hildreth was the first settler in 1770.

Liberty: In 1827, the area of Liberty was separated from Montville and the townspeople selected the name to show their love of liberty.

Lille: French for "island" describing the island in the St. John River.

Lily Bay: Named after lilies.

Limerick: James Sullivan was one of the first owners of the land in 1771 and named the town after Limerick, Ireland, his father's birthplace. Sullivan played important roles during the Revolutionary War. He was governor of Massachusetts while it still included Maine and wrote the first history of Maine in 1795.

Limestone: Named for limestone found in the area, the town was settled by General Mark Trafton in 1869.

Limington: Named either for Limington, Somersetshire, England or for Lymington, Hampshire, England. Ezra Davis was the first settler in 1773.

Lincoln: Around 1825, Enoch Lincoln bought some of the land in the area and the town was named for him. He became governor of Maine in 1827. It was first called Mattanawcook. Lincoln County was created in 1760 and its original borders went all the way north to Canada and east to Nova Scotia covering 3/5's of the District of Maine. The County's name honors Governor Thomas Pownall, who was governor of Massachusetts in the mid 1700s. His birthplace was Lincoln, England. Pownall was a supporter of American independence.

Lincolnville: General Henry Knox bought the land in 1792, but financial problems caused him to mortgage part of the area to General Benjamin Lincoln and General Henry Jackson in 1798. The town is named in honor of General Lincoln. Nathan Knight was the first settler in 1770.

Linekin: Benjamin Linekin was a settler in the mid 1700s.

Linneus: The land in this area was granted to Harvard College in 1804 to endow a botany professorship. Carolus Linnaeus was a famous Swedish botanist. The first settler came in 1826.

Lisbon: First called Thompsonborough after the Thompson family, who were large landowners. The townspeople petitioned to have the name changed to Lisbon, after the capital of Portugal, because they didn't like General Samuel Thompson's political views.

Litchfield: This area was first called Smithfield, and the townspeople requested the name Great Hampton when they incorporated in 1795. However, the General Court named it Litchfield instead, after the English town of that name.

Little Diamond Island: Named after Great Diamond Island.

Littlejohn Island: Probably named for John Cousins to differentiate Cousins Island from this island, as he owned both. There were also several families of that name who lived in the Yarmouth area.

Littleton: The land in this area was granted to Framingham Academy and Williams College around 1800. Josiah Little bought the Williams portion sometime before 1840 and the town is named after him.

Livermore: Named after Deacon Elijah Livermore, an early landowner and the first settler. It was originally called Oxford Royal, then Port Royal because the land had been granted to a number of people for their role in the expedition against Port Royal, Nova Scotia during the French and Indian War.

Lobster: The lake got its name from its shape. The other sites in the area got their names from the lake.

Locke Mills: Samuel Locke built a sawmill on this site in 1830, and the town is named after him.

Long: There are many lakes, ponds and other features with this name in Maine. It is typically descriptive of their length.

Lookout: Named for the point that serves as a lookout.

Loon Lake: Descriptive for the loons.

Lords Point: Tobias Lord was an early settler.

Louds Island: Named for island residents of that name.

Love Lake: John Love lived near the lake in the late 1700s.

Lovell: Captain John Lovewell was a great Indian fighter who was killed while defeating the Pequawket tribe under Chief Paugus in 1725 near Fryeburg. The soldiers and their heirs were given land on the Merrimac River called Suncook, but it ended up being in New Hampshire when the boundary was drawn. They were given land in Maine in the Lovell area instead and called it New Suncook. The name was later changed to Lovell in honor of Lovewell.

Lowell: First settled in 1819, the area was called Page's Mills and then Deanfield after Mary Dean, the first schoolteacher, and the Reverend Pindar Field. It was next called Huntressville after an early settler, and finally Lowell after Lowell Hayden, the first male child of one of the first settlers.

Lubec: French settlers first came from Nova Scotia in 1758, but soon moved to the upper St. John River. In 1776, people came from Nova Scotia who were sympathetic to the colonists during the Revolutionary War. There may have been some settlers from Germany too as the name comes from the German town of Lubeck.

Lucerne in Maine: Harold Saddlemire, who was developing the area, gave it this name for its similarity to Lucerne, Switzerland and to help promote land sales.

Luckse Sound: Unknown.

Ludlow: This land was granted to Belfast Academy and the town is named after Ludlow, Massachusetts.

Lyman: Incorporated as Coxhall in 1777, the name was changed in 1803 to honor Theodore Lyman, Esq. who began his career in Kennebunk and became one of Boston's most successful merchants.

Lynchville: Unknown.

M

Machias: The Indians called the river Mechises meaning "bad little falls" or "bad run of water." An English explorer mentioned the area on his map in 1527 and, the French had trading posts here until 1763 when the English gained control of the area and settlers began to move in.

Mackworth: Sir Ferdinando Gorges, the original proprietor, gave the point and island to Arthur Mackworth in 1631.

Macmahan: Terrence McMahan was a settler in the early 1700s.

Macwahoc: Abenaki for "wet ground" or "bog."

Madagascal: Abenaki for "meadows at the mouth."

Madawaska: Micmac for "where one river runs into another" or "having its outlet among the reeds." Another translator thinks it means "worn out grass." First settled in 1785 by French Acadians, the first American settlers came around 1817.

Madison: Named for President James Madison. Father Drueillette came through here in 1646 and Father Rasle lived here among the Indians, starting in 1695 until the English killed him in 1724. The first settlers came around 1774.

Madrid: First settled around 1807, legend says that a Spaniard was in town and asked for it to be named after the capitol of

Spain to honor its quest for freedom. It is more likely that is was named for Madrid because of the fashion of naming towns after foreign places in the early 1800s.

Maine: There is no definitive explanation about how Maine got its name, though there are several theories. One is that Charles I (King of England from 1625 to 1649) gave the name to honor his queen, Henrietta Maria of France, who supposedly owned the Province of Maine there. This has been quoted by many historians, but does not appear to be true. She did not have any relationship to the Province and, in addition, she married Charles in 1625, three years after he had granted all the land between the Merrimac and Kennebec Rivers to John Mason and Sir Ferdinando Gorges, using the name of Maine. Another theory is that it was named for the sea, often called by sailors "the main" or "the bounding main," because so much of the early history of Maine was tied to the sea. Similar to that theory is one that states that the earliest fishermen, working from the islands off the coast of Maine, were looking at the mainland (often spelled "maine land") and "Maine," a shortened version of mainland, stuck. James Rosier, who sailed with Bartholomew Gosnold in 1602 and George Waymouth in 1605 wrote, "From hence we might discern the maine land from the West-South-West to the East-North-East, and a great way…up into the maine we might discerne very high mountains." Gorges almost certainly read Rosier's accounts of these voyages. Lastly, one author asserts that Sir Fedinando Gorges, who is the Father of Maine, lived near a village settled by Frenchmen after the Battle of Hastings in 1066. Currently called Broadmayne, it was known as Maine in 1086. Sir Ferdinando's first ancestor to come to England was Ralph de Gorges who settled near Maine, England. The Gorges home is listed as being in Maine in the Domesday

Book, which is the census of England, according to this author. The Gorges' family records were destroyed during the English Civil War, so we may never know for sure where the name of Maine originated. It has been spelled Main, Mayne, and Mayn over the years until Maine became the standard spelling.

Malaga: Abenaki for "cedar."

Manana Island: This small island in Monhegan Harbor was called Manansis, which is Micmac for "small island." The name was corrupted over time to Manana.

Manchester: First called Kennebec at incorporation in 1850, the name was changed to Manchester in 1854 after Manchester, Massachusetts where some of the townspeople came from. It was first settled around 1774.

Mansell Mountain: Sir Robert Mansell owned land in the area.

Manset: Sir Robert Mansell was an early landowner and when the residents petitioned for a Post Office, a clerk mistakenly crossed the "l's" so they looked like "t's." The second "t" was later dropped. Another author thinks it is Abenaki for "at small island."

Maple Grove: Descriptive for maple trees there.

Mapleton: First settled around 1836, the town is named for the numerous maple trees.

Maquiot Bay: Abenaki for "a wet place."

Mariaville: Originally called Bingham after William Bingham of Philadelphia, who owned one million acres in Hancock and Washington counties. Bingham's daughter, Maria, had three marriages to noblemen from Europe and the town is named after her.

Marion: The name honors General Francis Marion, the "Swamp Fox" of Revolutionary War fame.

Marlboro: Named after Marlboro, England.

Marshfield: There were many marshes along the Machias River and Marshfield Stream and the name came from those. The British ship *Margueritta* hid in Marshfield Stream in the first naval battle of the Revolutionary War.

Mars Hill: A British Army Chaplain referenced Mars Hill in Athens, Greece, which the Apostle Paul mentions in the New Testament, while holding a service on this site around 1790. Moses Snow was the first settler in 1844.

Martinsville: Thomas Martin was an early settler and the town is named for his descendants.

Masardis: One source says Masardis means "place of white clay" in Abenaki and another says, "large stream." First settled by Thomas Goss in 1833.

Massachusetts: Maine was a part of Massachusetts from 1652 until statehood in 1820. The Massachusett were a tribe who lived at the base of Blue Hill in today's Milton, Massachusetts. Blue Hill is one of the tallest hills in Eastern Massachusetts, and the name means "great hill." Early settlers applied the tribe's name to the region.

Massacre Pond: Indians killed nineteen settlers here in 1702.

Mast Landing: Masts for the Royal Navy were collected here. Any pine 24 inches or more in circumference one foot off the ground belonged to the King and was marked with his sign to show ownership. A number of men made good money in the mast business.

Matagamon: Grand Lake Matagamon is Abenaki for "far on the other side."

Matinicus: Abenaki for "far out island."

Mattakeunk: Abenaki for "at end of swift stream."

Mattamiscontis: Abenaki for "alewife stream."

Mattanawcook: Abenaki for "at the end of the gravel bar."

Mattawamkeag: Abenaki for "fishing place beyond a gravel bar." Malecite for "rapids at mouth." Micmac for "on a sand bar." A cabin was built in 1829 to serve travelers, and Thoreau passed through here in 1847.

Mayfield: Unknown.

McGlathery Islands: The McGlathery family owned these islands.

Mechanic Falls: First called Jerico, then Groggy Harbor for the amount of grog sold there, then Bog Falls. In 1841, S. F. Waterman suggested the current name because of all the mechanics serving the factories in town.

Meddybemps: Passamaquoddy-Abenaki for "plenty of alewives."

Medford: This was the middle ford of the river. Med is a version of mid.

Medomak: Abenaki for "place of many alewives."

Medway: The Indians called this place Nicatow meaning "forks" because the east and west branches of the Penobscot meet here. It continued under this name until incorporation in 1875, when the name was changed to Medway (Midway) because it is halfway between Bangor and the northern boundary of Penobscot County.

Meduncook: Abenaki for "blocked by sandbars."

Meduxnekeag: Malecite for "falls or rapids at mouth."

Megunticook: Micmac for "big mountain harbor." This is the area around Camden.

Merchant Island: This island between Stonington and Isle au Haut is named for Anthony Merchant, who lived there during the Revolutionary Period.

Mere Point: John Mare was an early settler and it may be named for him. Others say it is from "mer," the French word for sea.

Merriconeag: Abenaki for "place for quick portage." Another translator says it means "lazy portage." The Indians would not unload their canoes and carry them, but would drag them across full.

Merrymeeting Bay: Probably named for the five rivers that meet there.

Messalonskee: Abenaki for "white clay here."

Metinic Island: Abenaki for "far out island."

Mexico: Named at incorporation in 1818 after the country of Mexico to honor its struggle for independence from Spain in the early 1800s.

Milbridge: First settled around 1763 by Joseph Wallace of Cape Elizabeth, who owned a ship and traded along the Maine coast. In the mid 1800s, a bridge was built across the Narragaugus River and a mill was built in town. The town's name comes from these two features.

Milford: A squatter settled here in 1800 and the area was called Sunkhaze, which is Abenaki for "concealed outlet." In 1833, the name was changed to honor Milford, Massachusetts where many of the settlers had previously lived.

Millimagassett: Abenaki for "where duckhawks abound."

Millinocket: One source says the name is Abenaki for "this place is admirable," and another says the name comes from the lake and means "dotted with many islands." Yet another says, "at the deep marsh grass." Thomas Fowler settled in the area around 1830.

Milo: Benjamin Sargent and his 14-year-old son came here in 1802. After building a cabin, the son, Theophilus, was left for the winter while the father returned to Massachusetts. The boy survived with the help of some local Indians and later named the town after Milo of Crotona, a Greek athlete.

Milton: Unknown.

Ministerial Island: The land was set aside for the use of the ministry.

Minot: Named to honor Judge Minot of the Massachusetts General Court in 1802 when the town was incorporated. It was first settled in 1769.

Minturn: Unknown.

Molasses Pond: An Indian woman named Molasses lived in the area.

Molunkus: Abenaki for "a ravine, high banks on each side."

Monarda: Unknown.

Monhegan: Micmac for "out to sea island." Captain George Weymouth gave the island the name of St. George in 1605. Its location usually makes it the first thing sailors see as they approach the coast of Maine. It is likely that many early explorers visited here and got water from the spring on Manana Island. Phoenicians may have visited it centuries ago as an inscription in Ogam carved on a rock on Manana reads, "Ships from Phoenicia. Cargo platform."

Monmouth: General Henry Dearborn lived here and was given 5,225 acres of land for his role in the Revolutionary War. He recommended the name in honor of the Battle of Monmouth during which he played a significant role.

Monroe: Named in 1818 for President James Monroe.

Montsweag: Abenaki for "narrow channel."

Moody Beach: The beach and point are named for Captain Samuel Moody, who was in the area in the early 1700s.

Monroe Island: Hugh Monroe owned this island.

Monson: This area was granted to Monson Academy of Monson, Massachusetts in 1807. A number of families moved from the Massachusetts town to the new town in 1819 and the name was given in honor of their old home.

Monticello: First settled in 1830, the town is named after Thomas Jefferson's estate in Virginia.

Montville: A descriptive name for the hills and mountains of the area. James Davis was the first permanent settler and so many of his relatives moved to the area that it was first called Davistown. The name was changed to Montville when it was incorporated in 1807.

Moody: Captain Samuel Moody was an Indian fighter in the early 1700s.

Moose: Many features are named after this magnificent animal.

Moosehead Lake: The origin is unclear but it may be that the name comes from viewing the lake from Mt. Kineo, and it looks like a moosehead, or that Mt. Kineo looks like a moose laying down when viewed from the lake, or for the many moose horns found there. The Indians called the lake "Seboomook," meaning "big lake."

Mooseleuk: Abenaki for "moose place."

Mooselookmeguntic: There are differing views on the Abenaki meaning. It could be "portage to the moose-feeding place," or "moose feeding among trees." Another source thinks it means "smooth when choppy seas." The "moose" at the beginning of the name either means "moose," or if it is "moosi" it means "smooth."

Mopang: Malecite for "solitary place."

Moro: Unknown.

Morrill: Originally part of Belmont, this area was split off in 1854 when the residents had trouble with the people from the southern part of Belmont. The town asked to be called Gilead, but was named after Maine's Governor Anson Morrill.

Morse: The features with this name in Phippsburg Township are named for David Morse, a settler in the mid 1700s. Morse Island in Muscongus Bay was named for another family named Morse.

Moscow: Named for Moscow, Russia in 1812 when Moscow was in the news because of Napoleon's military activity in the area.

Moshier Island: John Moshier was an early settler around 1660.

Mount Desert Island: In 1604, Samuel Champlain, sailing for the Sieur de Monts, who had been given a grant for Acadia by the King of France, sighted a number of mountains on a large island. He wrote, "It is very high, and notched in places, so that there is the appearance to one at sea, as of seven or eight mountains extending along near each other. The summit of most of them is destitute of trees, as there are only rocks on them....I named it Isles des Monts Deserts." In English that is, "Island of Barren Mountains." There is confusion about the proper pronunciation of Desert with visitors usually pronouncing it as it's spelled with the accent on the first syllable, and the locals and summer people pronouncing it as if it were spelled "dessert" with the accent on the second syllable. The Abenakis called it Pemetic.

Mt. Vernon: First settled in 1774, the name honors George Washington's estate in Virginia.

Mousam: Abenaki for "grandfather."

Moxie: May be Abenaki for "dark water."

Mud: Many Maine sites have this descriptive name.

Munjoy Hill. George Munjoy lived in the area in the mid 1600s. Peaks Island in Casco Bay carried his name for a while.

Munsungan: Abenaki for "humped up island."

Muscongus: Abenaki for "fish curing place." Another translator says, "many rocky ledges." The Indians first gave this name to an island in the bay, and then it was applied to the entire bay.

Musquacook: Abenaki for "muskrat place."

Musquash: Abenaki for "reddish, brown animal." It probably refers to a muskrat.

Mussel Ridge: Descriptive.

Myra: Luther Jackson moved here because there were no taxes at the time, and the town is named for his wife Elmyra.

N

Nahmakanta: Abenaki for "plenty of fish."

Naples: George Pierce first settled here in 1774 when he built a mill. He was a doctor and a lawyer too. The town was named after Naples, Italy.

Narraguagus: Abenaki for "above the boggy place."

Nash Island: The Nash brothers settled on these islands in the late 1700s.

Nash Lake: Amaziah Nash settled in the area.

Naskeag: Abenaki for "place at the end," which describes its location well.

Neddick: Micmac for "standing stone pillar." What it means is a nubble, a small rock in the sea.

Negro Island: Negro Island in Casco Bay is named for the many free blacks that lived in this area in the early 1800s. Negro Isiand near Boothbay is probably named for an African-American who lived there. Negro Island near Camden is named after a family's black cook who said that the island was hers as they went past the island in a boat.

Nesowadnehunk: Abenaki for "swift stream between mountains."

Newagen: It is an Anglicized form of "chawughnawaga," which means "swift current place."

Newburgh: The Scottish iteration of "town" is burgh and it was new, hence Newburgh.

Newcastle: First settled around 1630, the town is named for the Duke of Newcastle, who was the King of England's secretary around 1753 when the name was selected.

New England: First called Northern Virginia, Captain John Smith coined the name in 1614 while exploring Massachusetts and Maine. In 1616, he wrote a book about his travels called *A Description of New England*. The name was first used in an official document in 1620 when the charter creating The Council for New England stated, "The Council established at Plymouth in the County of Devon, for planting, ruling and governing New England in America."

Newfield: The name is descriptive for a "new field." Nathaniel Doe was the first settler in 1777.

New Gloucester: The General Court granted this land to 60 people from Gloucester, Massachusetts in 1735, and some of them settled here in 1742, but had to abandon the area during the Indian wars of 1741 to 1751. Some of them returned in 1753. For the next six years, the settlers slept at night in the fort they had built, and one of the men kept guard for Indians while they worked in the day.

New Harbor: The name is descriptive. John Brown settled here prior to 1625. The British attacked New Harbor during the War of 1812, but were repulsed.

New Limerick: This land was granted to the Phillips-Limerick Academy and many of the settlers came from Limerick in Southern Maine. The first settler came to the area in 1817.

New Meadows River: Named for the meadows in the area.

Newport: This town is on a path that was used by the Indians and the French missionaries for many years and the name comes from the "new portage" there between a river and Sebasticook Lake. First settled in the early 1800s.

New Portland: The General Court gave this land to the people of Falmouth in 1775 after their town was burned. Part of Falmouth went by the name of Portland and so the new town was named New Portland.

Newry: First called Sunday River and then Bostick, it was named Newry in 1805 as some of the settlers came from Newry, Ireland.

New Sharon: First settled around 1782, the town is named for Sharon, Massachusetts. The Plains of Sharon is a Biblical site.

New Sweden: This town was settled in 1870 by a group of emigrants from Sweden who named it after their homeland.

New Vineyard: People from Martha's Vineyard in Massachusetts settled this area in 1791 and named it after their old home.

Nicatous: Abenaki for "the little fork."

No Mans Land: No one wanted this valueless island.

Nobleboro: Probably named after James Noble, Esquire, who was an early landowner around 1730. The area was first settled as early as 1640.

Nonesuch: The name for this river, cove, and point may come from Nonsuch, the summer home of English royalty. Some say it may be for the river's erratic course or because there is, "'no such' land as good as this land."

Norcross: Nick Norcross was a lumberman in the area.

North: Descriptive.

Nollesemic: Abenaki for "resting place at the falls above the long stretch."

Norridgewock: Abenaki for "little falls and smooth water above and below." The Norridgewog Indians had a village here and the English killed the French missionary, Father Rasle, who had two chapels in the area during an attack on the village in 1724. The first settlers came in 1773.

North Amity: Settled in 1825 by Jonathan Clifford. Briefly called Monument Town as the monument designating the head of the St. Croix River is in the town. Also called Hodgdon for a while. Named Amity to honor the peace and harmony of the early inhabitants.

North East Carry: Named for a portage between Moosehead Lake and the West Branch of the Penobscot River.

Northeast Harbor: A descriptive name given because of its location on what should be called Mt. Desert Bay or Sound.

Northfield: The first settlers were from Machias around 1825. The name is descriptive for a large field north of Machias.

North Haven: Martin Pring, the English explorer, found this island in 1603 and called all the islands in the area the Fox Islands because of the many foxes found there. It was part of Vinalhaven for many years and was split off in 1846 and given its descriptive name then. People from Marshfield, Massachusetts settled it in the 1760s. The British forced some of the island residents to help them build fortifications during the Revolutionary War.

Northport: Named for its northern location in Penobscot Bay, it was first settled just before the Revolution.

North Yarmouth: Yarmouth is the name of a town in England and North was attached to distinguish the town from Yarmouth, Massachusetts. William Royall was probably the first settler around 1629. The river that runs through the town was originally called the Westcustego or Westgustego River, but the name was changed to Royall River to honor him. It was incorporated in 1680.

Norton Island: Named for the Nortons.

Norumbega: The Indians told early explorers about a city of gold, pearls, and jewels located up the Penobscot River. Giovanni Verrazano, exploring the coast of Maine in 1524, labeled the area above Penobscot Bay "Oranbega" on his map. The English, French, and others, interested in claiming what we today call Maine, hoped to find gold and silver just as the Spanish had in South America. In 1604, Champlain sailed up the Penobscot River to the present site of Bangor and discovered an Indian village, but no city of gold. One author says Norumbega is the

Old Spanish word for Northmen or Norsemen, and Maine got this name due to early visits from the Vikings. Some say it may be an Abenaki word. Various spellings of Norumbega were used on maps and in documents into the late 1600s to designate the area of Maine.

Norway: None of the early settlers, who came to the area in 1786, came from Scandinavia, so it wasn't named for the country. When the residents petitioned for incorporation around 1797, they asked that the town be called Norage, which was similar to the Indian word "norridge," meaning waterfall. The Legislature returned the name Norway, perhaps thinking they had misspelled Norge, the Norwegian spelling of Norway. One author thinks the Legislature did it to honor Norway, and another thinks they meant Norwich, but it was misspelled on the petition.

Notre Dame: Named after the famous church by Acadian settlers.

Nubble: A small rock, usually in salt water, that is too small to be an island, but large enough for several people to stand on. It has the same root as nub or nubbin, which means a knob, protuberance or stub.

O

Oakfield: There were fields surrounded by many oak trees in the area, so the oldest resident, James Timoney, gave it this name. This area stayed part of Massachusetts after 1820, becoming part of Maine in 1858.

Oakland: This town has had many names over the years, including Taconet and Kingsfield. It became part of Waterville and was incorporated as West Waterville in 1873. The name was changed to Oakland in 1883 as a descriptive name for oak trees growing there.

Ocean Park: Descriptive of its park-like setting on the ocean.

Ocean Point: Descriptive of its location.

Ogunquit: Abenaki word for "place of waves" or Micmac for "lagoons within sand dunes."

Olamon: Abenaki for "red paint." The Indians got ochre for painting their faces from the stream running through the town.

Old Orchard Beach: Thomas Rogers planted an orchard here in 1638. It became so well-known that the area was shown on old maps as "Rogers Garden." The Indian name for the bay was "Sowocotuck." Originally part of Saco, it was settled in 1631 by Richard Bonython. The beach is one of the longest beaches on the Atlantic coast.

Old Town: The site of an old Indian village named "Panawambske," the early settlers called it Old Town after that village. Richard Winslow was one of the first to settle here, building a sawmill in 1798.

Onawa: Chippawa for "awaken." Probably taken from Longfellow's poem, "Hiawatha."

Opechee Island: Chippewa for "robin."

Oquossoc: Abenaki for "slender blue trout."

Orient: Located on the eastern border of Maine, the town was called Orient denoting the word's meaning of "east." It was settled in 1830 and incorporated in 1856.

Orland: Legend says an early settler who found an oar on the shore of the river named it.

Orono: Named after an Indian chief, Joseph Orono, who was very helpful to the Americans during the Revolution. The son of a Frenchman and a woman of partial Indian heritage, Orono had blue eyes. Some question if the name is of Indian origin. First called Deadwater and then Stillwater, the area was first settled in 1774.

Orrington: When the townspeople met to discuss incorporation in 1788, a resident who had lived in Orangetown, Maryland suggested that name. The clerk wrote it down as "Orrington" and it was recorded that way.

Orrs Island: Named for Joseph Orr, a settler in the 1740s.

Otisfield: The land in this area was granted to the descendents of Captain John Gorham for his service fighting in Canada in 1690. It was named for Harrison Gray Otis, who was Mayor of Boston and a U.S. Senator from Massachusetts. Otis was one of Gorham's heirs and a major property owner in the area. Otis developed much of the land on Beacon Hill in Boston and several of his houses there, which were designed by Charles Bulfinch, are open to the public today.

Otter: Named for otters.

Ouellette: Named for an Acadian family.

Owls Head: The local Indians called this headland Bedabedec Point, meaning "cape of the winds." Some say the natives saw the resemblance and others that sailors saw the image in the mid 1750s and began calling it Owls Head.

Oxbow: Named for the oxbow shaped bend in the Aroostook River. It was settled in the 1840s.

Oxford: Named after Oxford County, within which it lies. David Leonard named the county for his previous home, Oxford, Massachusetts, which was named after Oxfordshire, England. The County was created in 1805.

P

Palermo: The town in Sicily inspired this name. Stephen Belden, Sr. was the first settler in the 1790s.

Palmyra: The second owner of the land in this area was Dr. John Warren. His son named the town after one of his sisters or it was named after the ancient Biblical city built by King Solomon. Dr. Warren was the brother of General Joseph Warren, who died at the battle of Bunker Hill. Dr. Warren also supported the Revolution, giving medical assistance to the Continental Army. Daniel Gale and his family were the first settlers in 1800.

Paris: The land in this area was granted to Joseph Fuller and his men for their service in the French and Indian War. It was named to honor Alfron Paris, who was a leader in the movement to separate Maine from Massachusetts, or after Paris, France, as it was popular to name towns after foreign cities and countries.

Parker Point: James Parker was a local innkeeper.

Parkman: Samuel Parkman of Boston bought the land in this area in the early 1800s, and the first settlers came in 1812.

Parlin: Unknown.

Parmachenee: Abenaki for "across the usual path." Legend says it was the name of an Indian chief's daughter.

Parsons Beach: Charles Parsons had a summer home here.

Parsonfield: Named for Thomas Parson, Esq.

Passadumdeag: Abenaki for "rapids over gravel beds." Settled in 1813.

Passagassawakeag: Malecite for "place for spearing sturgeon by torchlight."

Passamaquoddy: Abenaki or Micmac for "plenty pollock jumping," or "plenty pollock place."

Patten: A successful lumberman from Bangor named Amos Patten purchased the land here around 1830.

Peaks Island: The Palmer and Brackett families, who were killed by Indians in 1689, first settled this island. George Munjoy later owned the island and gave it his name. His widow married Samuel Peak and his name stuck. There was also a Joseph Peake who was in a Captain Jordan's Company in 1744, who lived in the area, but not on the island.

Pejepscot: Abenaki for "extended long rapids," or "extended rocky rapids."

Pemadumcook: Malecite for "extended sandbar place."

Pemaquid: Micmac for "extended land." Another meaning may be, "it is far out" (to the sea). This land was part of the Pemaquid Patent of 1631.

Pembroke: Jerry Burgin, Esquire, of Eastport gave this town a set of books for the right to name the town. He named it after Pembroke, Wales. Salt was imported from Pembroke, Wales to Pembroke, Maine where it was refined into table salt. Settled in 1774, the Indian name of the stream running through the area was Pennamaquam.

Pemetic Mountain: Abenaki for "range of mountains." Pemetic is the Abenaki name for Mt. Desert Island.

Pennamaquam: Abenaki for "sloping ridge of maples."

Penobscot: Indian word meaning "rocky part," "descending ledges," or "descending rocks." The name originally referred to the portion of the river between Old Town and Bangor. The tribe took its name from this part of the river, and the river, bay, and other features took their names from the tribe.

Perham: Named after Governor Sidney Perham, who was elected in 1871.

Perry: Incorporated in 1818, the town's name honors Commodore Oliver Perry who had won an important naval battle on Lake Erie against the British in 1813. Much timber from this area was sold to the British at great profit to the local lumbermen.

Peru: First called Partridgetown, the name commemorates Peru's independence from Spain in 1821, the same year the town was incorporated.

Petit Manan: Champlain named it after Grand Manan Island. The nearby point took its name from the island. It is one of the foggiest areas in America.

Pettingill Island: The Pettingill family lived on nearby Flying Point.

Phair: Thomas Phair owned starch factories in the 1880s.

Phillips: Jonathan Phillips of Boston owned the land prior to its incorporation in 1812.

Phippsburg: Named for Sir William Phipps, who became the royal governor of Massachusetts in 1692. One of 26 children born to one mother in Nauskeag, Maine (today's Woolwich,) he was a self-made man who was knighted for raising a Spanish treasure-ship wreck in the Caribbean.

Phoebe Island: Probably named for the type of bird with that name, though it could be named for a woman of that name.

Pickering Island: Samuel Pickering settled here.

Pierce: The origin of the name of the pond and surrounding sites in Somerset County is unknown.

Pine Point: Named for Charles Pines who lived in the area.

Pint Cove: Early pronunciation of "point."

Piscataqua: The river near Portland is Abenaki for "the place where the river divides." The river at the New Hampshire-Maine line is Pennacook Indian for "the place where the river divides."

Piscataquis: The county and features in central Maine are Abenaki for "a branch of the river," or "at the river branch." Piscataquis County was created in 1838.

Pistol: Unknown.

Pittsfield: Originally called Plymouth Gore, and then Warsaw, the name comes from William Pitts of Boston, who was a significant landowner.

Pittston: Named either for John Pitt, a member of the General Court from Boston in 1779 when it was incorporated, or for James Pitt, a Boston businessman, who was a proprietor of the Plymouth Company. Indians killed the first settler, Alexander Brown, in 1676.

Pittston Farm: The land was granted to Pittston Academy.

Plaisted: Governor Harris Plaisted was elected in 1881.

Pleasant: Many sites in Maine have this descriptive word in their names.

Plymouth: Named after Plymouth, Massachusetts, which is named after Plymouth, England.

Pocomoonshine: This name is either an Anglicization of an Abenaki word or a hybrid English-Abenaki word that means "pond as clear as moonshine."

Pocumcus: Micmac for "at the gravelly place."

Poland: Moses Emery was given the right to name the town when it applied for incorporation in 1795. It is thought that he named it after one of his favorite hymns called "Poland." However, there was an Indian chief in the area named Poland.

Pond: Many features have this descriptive name.

Popham Beach: The Plymouth Company was granted rights to all of present-day New England, and they sent two ships to colonize the area in 1607. They decided to build a settlement at the mouth of the Sagadahoc River, now called the Kennebec River, many years before the Pilgrims arrived at Plymouth, Massachusetts (1620). They built Fort St. George and named the settlement for the president of the colony, George Popham. He died that winter and the settlement was abandoned in 1608. The first ship built in New England, the *Virginia*, was built there and carried some of the colonists back to England that year.

Porcupine: Named for the animal.

Portage: The French word for "carry," it was named after a well-known portage in the area.

Port Clyde: The U.S. Post Office suggested the name for unknown reasons.

Porter Landing: Seward Porter ran a salt works here in the 1780s. He had 11 sons, several of whom were very successful in shipbuilding and the sea trade. They built and owned the *Dash*, one of the fastest and most successful privateers during the war of 1812, until it disappeared without a trace with several of the brothers aboard.

Portland: The Indians called the peninsula that includes the downtown area Machigonne, which is interpreted as, "shaped like a great knee." It may also mean "clay place." The first settlers were Richard Tucker and George Cleeve in 1633, who were granted the land by Sir Ferdinando Gorges. The area was first called Casco Neck, then Cleeve's Neck, and later Munjoy's Neck, as Cleeve sold his land to John Phillips in 1659 and his daughter married a Munjoy and inherited the land in 1681. For many years, it was called Falmouth and included the current towns of Cape Elizabeth, Falmouth, Westbrook, Portland, and Deering. The British burned most of Falmouth (Portland) to the ground during the Revolution. It took the name of Portland when it was incorporated in 1786. Cushing Island, just off Portland, was first called Portland Island, and a point on Cape Elizabeth was called Portland Head, and Portland was chosen over other suggestions such as Casco. Portland, England was the original source of the name. Portland became a city in 1832 and was the state capital from 1820 to 1831. A terrible fire in 1866 almost destroyed the city again. During World War II, a pipeline was built from Portland to Canada to send oil to refineries there. This allowed oil tankers to avoid additional exposure to U-boats as they steamed around the Maritime Provinces on their way to the St. Lawrence Seaway. The pipeline is still in use and all the tanks at the west end of Portland store the oil until it is sent through the pipeline.

Potato Island: Named for its shape.

Potts Harbor: Richard Potts lived in the area in the late 1600s.

Pound of Tea Island: An Indian traded the island for a pound of tea and perhaps several other things too.

Pownal: Thomas Pownal was governor of Massachusetts from 1757 to 1760. He was well respected and when the town was split off from Freeport in 1808, it was named for him.

Pratts Island: Ezra and Earl Pratt bought the island in the early 1900s and built summer cottages here.

Prebbles Point: Adam Preble oversaw the York Patent in the mid 1600s.

Prentiss: Originally called Deerfield, it is named for Henry Prentiss, a lawyer from Bangor, who owned the land in this area. It was settled in 1836 and incorporated in 1858.

Presque Isle: This name means "almost an island" in French, and its site between several rivers and streams makes the name an accurate one.

Presumpscot River: Abenaki for "ledges in channel."

Priestly: The lake and mountain in Piscataquis County are named for a man in the lumber business in the area with that last name.

Prince: Many features have this name, which usually came from a family of that name who settled in the area.

Princeton: First settled in 1815, the area is named for Princeton, Massachusetts.

Pripet: Unknown.

Prospect: Both Prospect and Prospect Harbor are named for the beautiful views from each of the towns.

Prouts Neck: Timothy Prout bought part of this area in 1728.

Pulpit Harbor: Named for the pulpit shape of a rock there.

Purgatory: Unknown.

Pushaw: Named for a local family with that name.

Q

Quahog: Natick Indian for "round clam."

Quakish: Abenaki for "flooded place." Micmac for "rough strewn."

Quimby: Unknown.

Quoddy: Short for Passamaquoddy, which means "pollock plenty place." Quoddy means "place."

West Quoddy Head Lighthouse

R

Rackliff Island: William Rackliff lived here around 1800.

Ragged: Descriptive. The Abenakis called this island near Matinicus Island "Raggertask," meaning "rock islands." The name was corrupted to "Ragged Ass," and then cleaned up to its present name.

Rainbow: The lake takes its name from its rainbow shape. The other sites are named for the lake.

Ram Island: Sheep were grazed on the island.

Randolph: Named after Randolph, Massachusetts, which is named for Peyton Randolph, the first President of the Continental Congress, who was from Virginia. It is the smallest town geographically in Maine.

Rangeley: Squire James Rangeley, an Englishman, bought the land in this area in 1825. He wanted to establish a great estate in the feudal style of landlord and tenants. He lived there with his family for about 15 years following the social customs of English nobility. The Hoar family was the first settlers in the area in 1817. Rangeley was incorporated in 1855.

Raymond: The heirs of Captain William Raymond and his company were granted the land in this area in 1767 for their service as members of Sir William Phipps Canadian expedition in 1690. Nathaniel Hawthorne grew up in Raymond.

Readfield: The local paper reported in 1903 that Readfield got its name because Peter Norton and his mother were avid readers. They lived there in the late 1700s.

Red Beach: Descriptive.

Reed: Settled in 1804, the origin of the name is unknown.

Reid State Park: Named for Walter E. Reid, a successful businessman who owned this land and gave it to the state in 1946 to become a park.

Richardson: The lake and other features in Oxford County are named for a family of early settlers in the area.

Richmond: Fort Richmond was built in this area in 1719, but was torn down in 1754. It was named for the Duke of Richmond, an Englishman who supported independence for the colonies. The town is named for the fort.

Richmond Island: This island off Cape Elizabeth is named for George Richmond, who settled there in the 1600s. Pierre du Guast, the Sieur de Monts, explored this island in 1605.

Ripley: Eleazer Ripley, a lawyer in Portland in the early 1800s, served in the Legislature. He fought in the War of 1812, distinguishing himself in battle. He never lived in Ripley. The town was incorporated in 1816.

Ripogenus: Abenaki for "gravel."

Riverside: Descriptive of its location.

Roach: The ponds and river are named for a type of sunfish called a roach.

Robbinston: Nathaniel and Edward Robbins owned land in the area.

Robinhood: Early settlers gave this name to a local Indian sachem. It was later applied to the area.

Rockland: This city was once a part of Thomaston and was first called Shore Village. Later it was called East Thomaston. The residents voted to change the name to Rockland in 1850, as the limestone quarries were a significant part of the town's business, along with fishing and timber. The Indians called the area "Catawamteak," which means "great landing place." The Lermond brothers were the first to log in the area in 1767, and the first settlers arrived in 1769.

Rockport: The Indians called the area "Megunticook," which means "big mountain harbor" or "swelling waves" in another dialect. The first settlers called it Goose Village after Goose River that flows into the bay here. As the town grew in size, the people decided a better sounding name than Goose Village was in order and in 1852 gave the town its current descriptive name for the rock-surrounded port. First settled in 1769, the area was part of Camden and wasn't incorporated as a separate town until 1891.

Rockville: Descriptive for the rock in the area.

Rockwood: Descriptive.

Rocky: Descriptive.

Rogue Island: Unknown.

Rome Corner: Originally called West Pond Plantation, this area was settled around 1780 and incorporated in 1804, when they named the town for the ancient city of Rome, Italy.

Roque: Roque Bluffs was part of Jonesboro until 1891 when it split off. The Bluffs is named for nearby Roque Island. There are several theories on where the name comes from. One is that it is a corruption of "rogues," as there was much smuggling in the area. The other is that Champlain named it St. Roch, and it was altered over time.

Round Pond: Descriptive.

Roxbury: Named after Roxbury, Massachusetts where some of the first settlers were from.

Royal River: William Royall lived in the area around 1629. His name was also spelled Royal, Ryall, Rial, and Riall.

Rum: The sites near Greenville got their name when a group of men drank a jug of rum and left the jug on the mountain. Other sites are unknown but probably had something to do with the consumption of rum.

Rumford: Concord, New Hampshire was originally called Rumford before the Revolutionary War. The Indians called it Pennacook. Sir Benjamin Thompson, Count Rumford, was knighted by the King in 1784 and, having lived in Concord, chose Rumford as his title after Concord's first colonial name. He was one of the proprietors of the land here. The plantation was called Pennacook or Pennycook, and the town was named after Count Rumford.

Russell: There are many features with this name. The mountains near Blanchard are named after a man named Russell who died on one of the mountains. The pond and surrounding sites with the same name are named after a lumberman named Russell. The rest are unknown.

Rutherford Island: Reverend Robert Rutherford lived here in the early 1700s.

S

Sabattus: Named for a chief of the Anasagunticook tribe who was killed in the area. It is said to be an Indian pronunciation of the French name, St. Jean-Babtiste.

Sabbathday Lake: A group of fur trappers met in this area to keep the Sabbath together.

Sabino: Named for an Indian sagamore.

Saco: Some say it is Abenaki for "flowing out," while other authors say it is not an Indian word. Estaban Gomez, who briefly explored the coast in 1525, named the bay, Bahia de Saco, or Bay of the Sack. Though Saco is now the name for the city, river, and bay, it was originally only used to designate the lower part of the river where it entered the ocean. This area had the first permanent settlement in Maine at the site of present-day Biddeford Pool. It was called Winter Harbor because Richard Vines and others wintered at that spot in 1616. The first organized government was here in 1635, and the settlements on both sides of the river were incorporated as Saco in 1653. The name was changed to Biddeford in 1718 after Bideford, England, and the part of the town on the east side of the river changed back to Saco in 1805.

Saddleback: The name is descriptive of the mountains near Rangeley and in Aroostook County. The names of other sites are also descriptive.

Sagadahoc: This was the original name the early explorers used for the Kennebec as that is what the Indians called the mouth of the river near the Popham Colony. It is an Abenaki word meaning "mouth of the river," or "place where strong current flows out." It was the eastern boundary of the Province of Maine in 1622. Sagadahoc County was split off from Lincoln County in 1854.

St. Agatha: Named for the parish church in the town that was named for St. Agatha, a third century martyr. It was incorporated in 1899 and was originally settled by Acadians.

St. Albans: Named for St. Albans, England, which was named for the first English martyr. St. Albans, England was a significant location in the events leading up to the Magna Carta.

St. Croix: Champlain named the river the St. Croix (Cross) because the Waweig River and the St. Croix form a cross where they meet in Oak Bay. Other sites are unknown, but may be taken from the river.

St. David: Named for the parish church in the town.

St. Francis: Unknown.

St. Froid Lake: Sefroi Nadeau was an early settler. St. Froid is a misspelling of his name.

St. George: Captain George Weymouth gave the name to the river and area in 1605. He named it after England's patron saint. He also called Monhegan Island, St. George Island. A blockhouse was constructed in 1630. St. George originally included the towns of Warren, Cushing, Thomaston, and St. George.

St. Helena Island: Named for the island where Napoleon was held prisoner. The quarry on the island used prisoners as laborers.

St. John: Samuel de Champlain named the river when he discovered it on St. John's Day in 1604. The town took its name from the river.

St. Sauveur Mountain: Named for the nearby French colony of that name in the 1600s.

Salem: A Biblical name, the Hebrew translates as, "complete, friendly, peaceable." First settled around 1815, the town was called North Salem after Salem, Massachusetts. When the town was incorporated in 1823, North was dropped from the name, as it was no longer necessary to distinguish between two towns of the same name in Maine and Massachusetts, now that Maine was a separate state.

Salisbury Cove: Ebenezer Salisbury was a settler in the area in the 1770s.

Sandy Creek: Descriptive.

Sandy Point: Descriptive.

Sanford: John Sanford, a governor of Rhode Island, and his descendants owned land in the area. It was first settled around 1740 and was incorporated in 1768.

Sangerville: Originally called Amestown after Phineas Ames who was the first settler around 1801. The name was changed to Sangerville to honor Colonel Calvin Sanger of Sherborn, Massachusetts who was the proprietor of the land in this area.

Saponac: Abenaki for "the great outlet" or "spread out water place."

Sargent Mountain: The Sargent family owned a large parcel of land on Mount Desert Island.

Sargentville: Named for the several families living in the area in the 1880s with the name of Sargent.

Sasonoa: The river and point are named for an Indian sachem of that name. Champlain met with Sasonoa when he explored this area in 1605.

Scarborough: This area was first settled around 1630 and was given its name in 1658 after Scarborough, England.

Schoodic: Either Abenaki or Malecite for "trout place" or "point of land." Another source thinks in means "opened by fire," meaning clearings of land.

Scraggly: The lake and brook's names are descriptive.

Seal Cove: Named for the seals in the area.

Seal Harbor: Named for the seals in the area.

Sears Island: David Sears owned much land in the area.

Searsmont: Originally called Greene after General Nathaniel Greene of Revolutionary War fame, it was called Searsmont after David Sears, the main proprietor of the area. Mont is derivative of mountain.

Searsport: David Sears was a proprietor along with several others who bought the land from the descendants of General Samuel Waldo. Originally part of Belfast and then Prospect, it was incorporated in 1845.

Seawall: A descriptive name for the rocks along the shore that create a natural sea wall.

Sebago: Abenaki for "big lake" or "a great water." The town is named after the lake and was first settled around 1790 and incorporated in 1826.

Sebasco: Abenaki for "almost through rock.

Sebascodegan Island: Abenaki for "carry or passage almost finished."

Sebasticook: Abenaki for "the shortest route."

Sebec: Abenaki for "much water" or "big lake," as its roots are similar to Sebago. This area was part of the grants made to Bowdoin College in 1794. Bowdoin sold this land to Richard Pike in 1803. The town was incorporated in 1812.

Seboeis: Abenaki for "small lake" or "little stream."

Seboomook: Abenaki for "big lake" or "at or near the large stream."

Sedgwick: Major Robert Sedgwick of Charleston, Massachusetts was a soldier who fought successfully against the Indians and the French in the 1600s. He helped capture three important French trading posts including present-day Castine. Andrew Black was the first permanent settler in 1759.

Seguin Island: Abenaki for "humped up" or "turtle." This refers to its turtle-like shape.

Seven Hundred Acre Island: Descriptive of its size.

Shallow Lake: Descriptive.

Shapleigh: Major Nicholas Shapleigh of Kittery was the main proprietor of the area. It was first settled in 1772 and incorporated in 1785. Shapleigh bought the land from an Indian sagamore named Captain Sunday.

Shawmut: Shawmut is the Indian name of the peninsula that Boston was established on in 1630. The mills in this area were bought by a group of Boston investors whose offices were on Shawmut Street and they gave that name to the town.

Sheep Porcupine Island: First called "She Porcupine Island," it changed over time to its present name.

Sheepscot: Abenaki for "many rocky channels," "at the split rock," or "divided by many rocks."

Sheridan: Named for General Phillip Sheridan, the Civil War general, by a man who served under him in the war.

Sherman: Senator John Sherman of Ohio, who was also Secretary of State and Treasury, is honored with this name.

Shin Pond: Named for a local lumberman.

Ship Island: At one point it looked like a ship being pulled by two barges: nearby West Barge Island and East Barge Island.

Shirley Mills: Joseph Kelsey, Esquire, the local legislator in 1834, named the town after his birthplace of Shirley,

Massachusetts, which was named for Governor William Shirley.

Sidney: Incorporated in 1792, Sidney is named for Sir Philip Sidney, an English war hero and distinguished poet of the sixteenth century.

Sieur de Monts Spring: Pierre du Guast, the Sieur de Monts was granted the land of "La Cadie" by the King of France in the early 1600s. He and Champlain explored the coast of Maine in 1604 and 1605.

Silvers Mills: A family named Silvers owned the local lumber mill.

Sinclair: Unknown.

Skowhegan: This area was originally part of Canaan, but was split off in 1823 and initially called Milburn. In 1836, the name was changed to Skowhegan, the area's Indian name, which means "place of the watch" or "watching place for fish." The Indians would camp here to spear salmon as they migrated up the river to spawn. The fish would rest before making their way up the falls. Benedict Arnold and his men camped here on their famous expedition to Canada.

Small Point: The point and beach near Popham are named for John Small, a surveyor.

Smithfield: The town was named for one of its residents, Reverend Henry Smith, when it was incorporated in 1840.

Smithville: Unknown.

Smuttynose Island: Named for a prominent black ledge that contrasts with the surrounding lighter colored rock.

Smyrna Mills: Named for the ancient city of Smyrna in Asia Minor, known today as Turkey. It was settled in 1830 by Nehemiah Leavitt and was incorporated in 1839.

Sodom: A group of railroad workers lived in rail cars here and were given to much drinking and partying. The area people gave the name after the Biblical city that represents wickedness.

Soldier Pond: During the Aroostook War, which began in 1837 over disputed land claimed by both Maine and New Brunswick, some soldiers built short-term quarters near this site.

Solon: Named after Solon, an ancient Greek statesman. The name has come to mean "a wise lawgiver." It was settled in 1782.

Somerset: Sir Ferdinando Gorges received several large grants of land in Maine in the early 1600s. His home was in Somerset County in England, and he briefly called his grant New Somersetshire. However, the King wouldn't allow it and insisted it be called the Province of Maine. Somerset County was broken off from Kennebec County in 1809, and the new county was named after the English county. Much of the Bingham Purchase was in Somerset County.

Somerville: Unknown.

Somesville: Abraham Somes was an early settler in the area in the 1760s. He made his living cutting barrel staves.

Somes Sound: Abraham Somes settled at the head of the sound in the 1760s. Somes Sound was once thought to be a fjord, but is not considered to be one today.

Songo: Abenaki for "the outlet."

Sorrento: Named for Sorrento, Italy, which has beautiful views across the Bay of Naples, just as Sorrento, Maine has beautiful views across Frenchman Bay. The Indians called the area Waukeag, which means "a great knoll," and the French called it Douaquet when they controlled the area in the 1600s.

South Arm: Descriptive for its location on the south arm of Richardson Lake.

Southport: This town was originally part of Boothbay. When it was split off in 1842, it was given the name of Townsend, which was the original name of the plantation encompassing that area. The residents asked the Legislature to change the name to Southport in 1850 to avoid confusion with Boothbay, which was also known as Townsend because that was the historical name of the area.

Southwest Harbor: The name is descriptive for its location at the southwest corner of Mt. Desert Island. The Jesuits first made a settlement here in 1615, and the area has been inhabited since then, though it wasn't incorporated until 1905.

Sow and Pigs: These islands were given their names by some-one who thought they looked like their namesakes.

Spaulding: Charles Spaulding lived in the area in the early 1900s.

Spectacle: The islands and pond are named for their eyeglass-like shape.

Spednik: Abenaki for "visible, but shut in by mountains."

Spencer: The lake and mountain in Somerset County are named after a lumberman of that name. The sites in Piscataquis County are named after another lumberman.

Spider Lake: Unknown.

Spoon Island: Named for its shape.

Springfield: Either named for Springfield, Massachusetts, or it is a descriptive name for the fields and springs in the area. First settled around 1830, the town was incorporated in 1834. The Burr family settled there first.

Spring: Named for the springs that feed the lakes, rivers, streams, and ponds.

Springvale: Legend has it that during a meeting to discuss what to call the town, a man got up and pointed to the nearby spring and then pointed to the valley, saying, "spring" and "vale" when pointing to each. It is probably descriptive.

Spruce Head: Descriptive for the spruce trees growing there.

Spurwink: Unknown, though possibly for an early settler.

Squa Pan: Abenaki for "bear's den." Also Squapan.

Square Lake: The Indian word meaning "round' was mistranslated to "square."

Squirrel: Many sites are named after squirrels.

Stacyville: Named for James Stacy, its first settler. It was incorporated in 1953.

Stage Island: The island, harbor and other features were named for the fish drying racks, called "stages," used on the island.

Standish: This area was granted to Captains Humphrey Hobbs and Moses Pearson and their men for their service during the siege of Louisbourg. Originally named Pearsontown after Captain Pearson, the name was changed to Standish when it was incorporated in 1786 to honor Miles Standish, one of the Pilgrims of Plymouth Plantation.

Staples: The cove and point on Cape Elizabeth are named for a family that lived there in the mid 1800s. The point and cove in Falmouth are named for Joseph Staples, who lived there in the 1700s.

Starboard: Named for the nautical term meaning "on the right."

Starks: General John Starks fought at Bunker Hill and at the Battle of Bennington during the Revolution. James Waugh was the first settler. It was called Sandy River Plantation until it was incorporated as Starks in 1795.

State Road: A state road was built from Presque Isle to Ashland in 1842 and the name came from that.

Stave Island: Barrel staves were made on the different islands with this name.

Steels Harbor Island: The Steele family settled on the island.

Steep Falls: Descriptive.

Stetson: This area was originally granted to Leicester Academy in 1791. After being sold to several owners, Amasa Stetson of Dorchester, Massachusetts bought it and the town is named for him.

Steuben: Friedrich Wilhelm Augustus, Baron von Steuben was a German who helped during the Revolution by drilling Washington's untrained troops during the winter they were at Valley Forge. He was the Inspector General of the Continental Army. The town is named for him. It was settled in 1760 and incorporated in 1795.

Stickney Corner: Named for the Stickney family.

Stillwater: Named because the waters of the Penobscot River flow slower here than in most places.

Stinson Point: Thomas and Samuel Stinson settled here and on the neck in the mid 1700s.

Stockholm: Named for the capital of Sweden by Swedish emigrants, who settled the area in 1881.

Stockton Springs: Originally a part of Prospect, the town was spilt off in 1857 and was named Stockton after Stockton, England. In 1889, the name was changed to Stockton Springs because the townspeople hoped a spring there would prove to be profitable.

Stonington: First called Green's Landing, the name was changed to Stonington in 1897 when it was incorporated. The name honors the incredible granite quarries of the area. Home to some of the greatest quarries in the world, Stonington granite has been used in many cities including Boston and New York. Crotch Island granite was used to build the Museum of Fine Arts in Boston.

Stow: Named for Stow, Massachusetts, the area was settled in the 1770s and incorporated in 1833. The Pequaket Tribe lived in this area.

Stratton: Named for an early settler.

Strong: Previously called Readsville after an early landowner, the name was changed to honor the then sitting governor of Massachusetts, Caleb Strong, when the town was incorporated in 1801.

Stroudwater: Named for Stroudwater, England.

Sturdivant Island: Named for a settler of that name.

Sugarloaf Mountain: Named for its shape. Often names with "sugar" in them have had maple sugar operations associated with them.

Sullivan: This area was first settled around 1762 and was incorporated in 1789 when it was named for Captain Daniel Sullivan, an early settler. In 1776, he built a blockhouse near his home and organized a company of men for the War. One of his brothers was governor of Massachusetts and another governor of New Hampshire.

Sumner: First settled in 1783 by former Revolutionary War soldiers who came from the Pembroke, Massachusetts area. When the town was incorporated in 1798, they named it for the incumbent governor of Massachusetts, Increase Sumner.

Sunday River: The river was discovered on a Sunday.

Sunset: Descriptive of its location on the western side of points and islands where you can watch the sunset.

Sunshine: Descriptive.

Surry: When the town petitioned to be incorporated, they asked that they be given a short name, such as Kent or Surry. The General Court chose Surry after Surrey, England and even omitted the "e" in Surrey to make it shorter. The first settlers came in 1767 and the town was incorporated in 1803. Leonard and Philip Jarvis began buying land in the area and were the second largest landowners in the state by 1800.

Swan Island: This island in the Kennebec was named for James Swan who fought in the Revolutionary War and owned the island.

Swan Lake: Named for the early settlers with that name.

Swans Island: Colonel James Swan bought Burnt Coat Island in 1786 and built a big mansion there. Champlain called the island Brule-Cote, which means "burnt coast" in French, but it was mistakenly called "burnt coat" by the English. Swan emigrated from Scotland in 1865 and settled in the Boston area. He was a vigorous supporter of American independence and participated in the Boston Tea Party, fought at Bunker Hill, and was close to Washington and Lafayette. While in France as an agent buying American goods for the French government, he was arrested and put into debtor's prison by the French in 1808 and spent 22 years there because he refused to pay the debt, claiming he had not incurred it. He died three days after being released. The island was incorporated in 1897 as Swan's Island, though the primary harbor is still called Burntcoat Harbor.

Swanville: Named for early settlers named Swan. When the town petitioned the General Court for incorporation, they added "ville" to the name.

Sweden: Named for the country of Sweden after the popular act of naming towns for foreign places in the early 1800s. There is also a Sweden just next to New Sweden in Aroostook County that was given that name because Swedish immigrants settled it.

Sysladobsis: Malecite for "rock shaped like a dogfish."

T

Tarantine Station: Unknown.

Telos: In Greek it means "the end," "far," or "ultimate."

Temple: Named after Temple, New Hampshire where some of the early settlers came from around 1796. It was a strong Quaker community.

Tenants Harbor: Probably named for Joshua Tenant, though it is unclear as some feel the name precedes him.

Third: Descriptive.

Thomaston: First settled in 1736, the town is named for General John Thomas who served in the Revolutionary War. Washington had him help prepare Dorchester Heights, and he commanded the American troops in Canada. The town's most famous early resident was General Henry Knox, George Washington's first Secretary of War. He led the expedition that brought the captured British cannons from Fort Ticonderoga to Boston, which were instrumental in forcing the British to leave Boston in the early part of the war. He built a great mansion in Thomaston in 1793-94, which was torn down in the 1870s. A replica was built later and can be seen today from Route 1.

Thompson: The lake is named for a man named Thompson who drowned while crossing it. The sites near Hartford are named for four men named Thompson.

Thorndike: Israel Thorndike was a successful businessman from Boston who commanded several privateers during the Revolution. He was one of the proprietors who bought this area in 1806. He built a large farm here.

Thread of Life ledges: Named for the narrow ships' channel that runs through the middle.

Thrumcap Island: A thrumcap is a cap made of rope by a sailor. Some sailors thought the island looked like one.

Thunder Hole: The water rushing into the hole sounds like thunder.

Tim: These sites in Franklin County are reputedly named for a hunter named Tim.

Tinker Island: The Tinker family bought the island for a keg of rum.

Todds Corner: Unknown.

Toddy Pond: Toddy is slang for liquor. The pond in Hancock County got its name because someone used the water from the pond to make liquor. The pond near Blue Hill got its name when a British soldier dropped his liquor into the lake while crossing it.

Togus: Abbreviated form of the Abenaki "Worromontogu," which means "brook entering cove."

Topsfield: Nehemiah Kneeland settled here in 1832. He came from Topsfield, Massachusetts and gave that name to the new settlement.

Topsham: Named for Topsham, England. The first settlers came in 1669, but were killed by Indians.

Town Hill: The town owned several hundred acres on the hill.

Trap Corner: Legend says that Ebenezer Drake built a store here to "trap" business that was going elsewhere.

Tremont: This town is named for three mountains in the area. It is from the French, "tre" or "tri" for three and "mont" for mountain. The Puritans who settled Boston in 1630 first saw land here after their Atlantic crossing and called the mountain Mt. Mansel.

Trenton: Settled around 1763 and incorporated in 1789, the town is named to commemorate the Battle of Trenton, which took place in Trenton, New Jersey, December 26, 1776. The Battle of Trenton was an important victory for the Americans, giving hope after a series of loses to the British.

Trial Point: This point on Isle au Haut was given its name because it was a trial for a boat to get past it into Moore Harbor.

Trott Island: John Trott owned the island in the 1600s.

Troy: This town had many names before selecting the current name. It was originally called Bridgestown after General Bridge, the proprietor. Next, it was incorporated as Kingsville to honor Governor William King, and then Joy after Benjamin Joy, a Boston merchant and proprietor. Later, it was called Montgomery in honor of General Richard Montgomery, the

American general who was killed at the battle of Quebec during the Revolutionary War. Finally, it was named Troy after the ancient city in modern-day Turkey, as classical names were in vogue.

Trout: This name is attached to many sites and is descriptive of the fish.

Tunk Lake: Probably Abenaki for "large swift stream."

Turner: The town is named for the Reverend Charles Turner, who graduated from Harvard in 1752 and preached in Duxbury for many years. He worked in several capacities for the proprietors of the area and later moved to Turner as a part-time preacher. There are ponds and other features whose names come from local settlers or lumbermen.

Twin: The lakes and other sites have a descriptive name.

Two Bush: The island near Matinicus Island was given this descriptive name and the channel is named after the island. Other islands have the same name, which is descriptive.

U

Ugh Lake: Unknown.

Umbagog: Abenaki for "clear lake."

Umbazooksus: Abenaki for "clear, gravelly outlet."

Umculcus: Abenaki for "whistling duck."

Umsaskis Lake: Abenaki for "linked together like sausages."

Union: First settled in 1774, the town was called Taylortown after Dr. John Taylor, the proprietor of the area. Later, it was called Sterlington when it was incorporated in 1786. A few months later, the residents changed the name to Union to reflect how well they all got along.

Union River: In the mid 1700s, a shipload of settlers had trouble agreeing where to land to start their settlement. After discussing it and reaching agreement, they sailed up what they called the Union River because of their unity.

Unionville: Three roads came together here "in union."

Unity: Settled around 1782, the town was first called Twenty-five Mile Pond. In 1804, it was incorporated as Unity to reflect the political unity the town had, which was Democrat at the time. The pond took its name from the town.

Upper Gloucester: See New Gloucester.

Upton: Named for Upton, Massachusetts, which was named for Upton, England. It is near Grafton, Maine just as Upton, Massachusetts is near Grafton, Massachusetts.

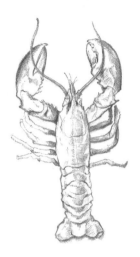

V

Vaill Point: The Vaill family lived here for many years.

Van Buren: Incorporated in 1881, the town is named for President Martin Van Buren, who was president during the Aroostook War.

Vanceboro: William Vance owned large tracts of land in this area and elsewhere in Maine. He was from Baring, south of Vanceboro, and was a delegate to the state Constitutional Convention of 1819.

Vassalboro: Settled around 1760 by people from the Cape Cod area. Settlers after 1780 were mostly Quakers from New York. The town is either named for a proprietor of the Plymouth Company from London, Florentine Vassall, or for William Vassal of Massachusetts. Several captains of whalers from Nantucket moved to Vassalboro around 1827.

Vaughns Island: The Vaughn family owned the island in the 1800s.

Veazie: General Samuel Veazie owned sawmills in the area. He fought in the War of 1812. It was part of Bangor until it was incorporated in 1853.

Verona: It was first called Penobscot Island, then Wetmore's Island and next, Orphan Island, because it was all the land that General Henry Knox had left to bequeath to his orphan grandchildren. The town was incorporated in 1863 and is named after Verona, Italy. This was not because any settlers came from there, but due to the fashion of the time to name cities after foreign places.

Vienna: Named for Vienna, Austria (part of Germany then), due to the custom of naming towns for foreign places. It was first settled around 1786, and was incorporated in 1802.

Vinalhaven: The English explorer, Martin Pring, visited these islands in 1603 and called them the Fox Islands for all the foxes found here. Vinalhaven was South Fox Island and North Haven was North Fox Island. Vinalhaven is named for John Vinal, Esq., who helped island residents with legal work regarding their land titles. First settled in the 1760s, Vinalhaven was incorporated in 1789. North Haven, originally part of Vinalhaven, was split-off in 1846.

W

Waite: Benjamin Waite was a lumberman from Calais. People from Calais settled it in the 1830s.

Waldo: Waldo is a renowned name in the history of Maine. In 1630, John Beauchamp and Thomas Leverett were granted a large tract of land in mid-coast Maine, which was called the Muscongus Patent. By the early 1700s, ownership had descended to Thomas Leverett, the president of Harvard, and 10 others. They hired Samuel Waldo, the son of a minor German nobleman (the family name was originally Von Waldow) to serve as their agent for land sales. He convinced settlers to come to the area and was successful in blocking the English Privy Council from granting part of the land to another group. In 1719, Samuel Waldo was given half of the Patent for these services he had performed. He later bought the rest of it, and it became known as the Waldo Patent. His granddaughter married General Henry Knox, who then inherited much of this land. Waldo was first settled in the early 1800s and was incorporated in 1845. Waldo County was separated from Hancock County in 1827.

Waldoboro: Samuel Waldo owned the Waldo Patent. General Waldo convinced some German and Irish immigrants to settle here in the 1740s, but Indians wiped-out the town. In the 1850s, the General's son persuaded many people to emigrate from Germany. The town was first called Broad Bay and General Waldo built a fort there. The town was later named for him. Be sure to eat at Moody's Diner.

Walkers Point: The Walkers first settled in Maine in the 1600s, and Richard Walker settled in the area of Walker's Point in the 1740s. They became a very successful, influential family eventually producing two Presidents of the United States: George Herbert Walker Bush and George W. Bush. The first President Bush's mother was a Walker. In the early 1900s, the Walkers built the big house on Walkers Point that is now the summer home of the first President Bush.

Wallagrass: Abenaki for "shallow, full of holes." Micmac for "good river."

Walpole: Possibly named after Walpole, Massachusetts, which was named for Walpole, England. It may have been named for one of several noted Englishmen of the 1700s with that surname.

Waltham: Named for Waltham, Massachusetts. For many years, the only way to get to the town was by boat on the Union River. It was settled around 1804 and incorporated in 1833.

Warren: Settled in 1736, the town was first called Upper St. George. Upon incorporation in 1776, it changed its name to honor General Joseph Warren, who died a hero at the Battle of Bunker Hill. General Waldo had some of his enterprises in the area, including a gristmill, lime kilns, and others.

Warren Island: Samuel Warren owned the island.

Washburn: Governor Israel Washburn was governor during part of the Civil War and had previously served in Congress for ten years.

Washington: First named Putnam to honor General Israel Putman, a Revolutionary War general, the town changed its name in 1823 to honor President George Washington. Hancock and Washington Counties were split off from Lincoln County in 1789 as more people settled down east after the Revolution.

Wassataquoik: Abenaki for "a clear shining lake."

Wassookeag: Abenaki for "shining fish place." It probably refers to fishing by torchlight.

Waterboro: Colonel Joshua Waters was one of the early proprietors of the area. It was originally called Massabesic Plantation. Major William Phillips originally bought this land from several Indian chiefs in the 1660s.

Waterford: The town is named for a shallow part of the Crooked River used as a ford. The first settler came in 1775.

Waterville: The name is descriptive of its location on the Kennebec River. It was originally part of Winslow, which is across the river, but they were separated in 1802 when it was incorporated as Waterville. The Indian name for the area was Ticonic, which means "a place to cross."

Waukeag: Abenaki for "a great knoll."

Wayne: The name honors General Anthony Wayne, one of George Washington's great generals during the Revolutionary War.

Webb: The lake and river in Franklin County got their name when a group of men exploring the area found the name "Thomas Webb" carved in a tree near here.

Webhannet: Abenaki for "at the clear stream."

Webster Head: The Webster family settled in the area in the mid 1700s.

Webster Lake: Unknown.

Weeks Mills: Major Abner Weeks built a sawmill and a gristmill here.

Welchville: John Welch of Boston was an early proprietor.

Weld: The land in this area was first purchased by Jonathan Phillips in the late 1700s and sold to three men, including Benjamin Weld of Boston, in 1815. They sold land to settlers.

Wellington: First settled in 1814 and originally called Bridge's Town for an early proprietor, the name honors the Duke of Wellington who defeated Napoleon at the Battle of Waterloo in 1815.

Wells: Sir Ferdinando Gorges, a proprietor of the Plymouth Company, which had the charter for much of Maine, was from Somersetshire, England. Some historians think that he personally named Wells after the English city of Wells near his home in England. It was the third town to be established in Maine and was settled around 1642. The first settler was Reverend John Wheelwright who had been banished from Massachusetts for his religious beliefs.

Weskeag River: Shortened form of an Abenaki word meaning "tidal creek at the peninsula.

Wesley: John Wesley was the founder of Methodism.

West: This is a descriptive name.

Westbrook: This area was originally part of Old Falmouth, which included the present areas of Portland, Falmouth, Cape Elizabeth, Deering, and Westbrook. Westbrook was first called Stroudwater by Colonel Thomas Westbrook. Westbrook was an interesting man who was responsible for obtaining masts for the Royal Navy. This activity was relocated from Portsmouth, New Hampshire to Falmouth in 1726. The Crown laid claim to every pine tree greater than 24 inches in diameter one foot off the ground. He commanded troops during the Fourth Indian War and went on to be a successful businessman. One of his many accomplishments was building the first paper mill in Maine in this town. The name was changed from Stroudwater to Westbrook in his honor in 1814.

Westfield: The town is named for Westfield, Massachusetts. This land was granted to Deerfield Academy and to Westfield by the State of Massachusetts to support their educational institutions. James Thorncraft first settled here in 1839.

West Forks: Descriptive of its location at the fork of the Kennebec and Dead rivers.

Weston: Named for the manwho surveyed the town in 1835. The land was originally granted to Hampden Academy in Maine in 1803.

West Point: Descriptive.

Westport: The area was first called Jeremisquam, which seems to be a hybrid Indian and Anglo word. "Misquam" means "a great neck," according to Fannie Eckstorm, a noted scholar of Indian languages, and she comments that no one knows what the first part signifies. My research shows that the land around Wiscasset, and perhaps down the river this far, came to be owned by a group of wealthy Boston merchants who put their rights into a company called, "The Boston or Wiscasset Co." Later, the name was changed to "Wiscasset and Jeremy Squam Proprietors." I have been unable to find out if Jeremy Squam was a person or if it is an Indian word, and the name remains a mystery. Westport was originally part of Edgecomb, but was separated in 1828 and given its present name because it was the port in the western part of Edgecomb. An Indian named One Robinhood sold this area to John Richards in 1649.

Whaleboat Island: The island looks like a whaleboat to some.

White: Islands and other sites are named for their light color.

Whitefield: George Whitefield, a popular minister from England, visited Maine in 1745.

White Horse Lake: Unknown.

Whiting: When the town was incorporated in 1825, the towns-people voted to name the town after Timothy Whiting, a highly thought-of resident. He gave 400 acres to the town to be used to support the town's schools. It was first settled by John Crane who had served with distinction throughout the Revolutionary War, ending up a Brigadier-General in 1793. He moved to the area after the war.

Whitmore Neck: Joseph Whitmore settled here.

Whitneyville: The town is named for Colonel Joseph Whitney, a successful businessman in the area, when it was incorporated in 1845. It was part of Machias until then.

Willard Beach: Named for Captain C. Willard.

Willimantic: This area was never opened to settlement, but was kept for commercial uses such as lumbering and quarrying. It was first called Howard after an early proprietor. In 1883, the name was changed to Willimantic after Willimantic, Connecticut. The Willimantic Thread Company had opened a mill here to make thread spools. In Abenaki, it means "a good watch place on the stream." The company was from Connecticut and already had the name when they came to Maine. In the Mohegan dialect it means "wide range lookout."

Wilson Pond: The pond and other features in Piscataquis County were named for a man named Wilson, who was one of the first into this area.

Wilsons Mills: Named for a mill owner named Wilson.

Wilton: This area was granted to Captain William Tyng and his men for their victory against some Indians in a battle in 1703. It was first called Harryville, to honor one of the Indians killed in the battle, and then Tyngston after Captain Tyng. When the town was incorporated in 1803, it was named Wilton after Wilton, New Hampshire, the hometown of an early settler.

Windham: This area was granted to a number of people from Marblehead, Massachusetts in 1734 and was called New Marblehead. The town was incorporated in 1762 as Windham. No one is certain why, but it is thought that it is named after Windham, Norfolk, England.

Windsor: This town went through several names before settling on Windsor to honor the Royal Family of England and Windsor Castle. It was first called Malta after the island in the Mediterranean Sea, and then Gerry after Elbridge Gerry, a governor of Massachusetts and Vice President of the United States in the early 1800s. It was first settled around 1790 and incorporated in 1809.

Winn: First called Snowville after Joseph Snow who settled in the area in 1820, and then Five Islands, the town was incorporated in 1857 as Winn after John Winn of Salem, Massachusetts, who had bought the land but lost it due to financial troubles.

Winslow: Fort Halifax, named for the Earl of Halifax, was built in 1752 at this site. It would hold 400 men to defend against Indian attacks. The town was first called Kingfield, but was incorporated as Winslow in 1771 after General John Winslow, who had commanded the men who built the fort.

Winslows Mills: Named for John Winslow.

Winter Harbor: Originally part of Gouldsboro, Winter Harbor was split off in 1895. It got this name because the harbor is used throughout the winter, as it doesn't freeze up. It was first called Mosquito Harbor.

Winterport: This area was part of Frankfort until a dispute over who should pay for the annual repairs to the bridge across the Marsh River caused a separation. Winterport's name is descriptive, as the Penobscot River remains free of ice in this area in the winter.

Winterville: Uncertain, but probably descriptive.

Winthrop: This area was first settled in 1760 and was called Pondtown. It was incorporated in 1771 and named Winthrop to honor John Winthrop, the first governor of the Massachusetts Bay Colony.

Wiscasset: Abenaki for "the outlet" or "at the hidden outlet." John and George Davie of England and several others were the first settlers in 1660 and bought the land from some Indian chiefs. The settlers fled for their lives at the outbreak of King Philip's War in 1675, and their homes were burnt. A group of wealthy Boston merchants gained ownership of the land in 1734, and settlement began anew. Robert Hooper and family were the first to settle this time. A fort was built on Fort Hill in the 1730s for protection from Indians. The area was part of Pownalborough until 1802 when it was split off and incorporated as Wiscasset.

Wohoa Bay: Fisherman shouted this sound to each other when lost in the fog.

Wolfes Neck: Henry Wolf settled in the area around 1671.

Wood: A number of features have this name, which is descriptive.

Wooden Ball Island: The highest point looks like a round ball. It used to be covered by trees.

Woodland: First settled in 1860 by people from Massachusetts, and in 1872 by Swedish immigrants, the name is descriptive for its location in the woods.

Woolwich: The area was purchased from the Indians in 1638 and is named for Woolwich, England.

Wreck Island: This island off Stonington is named for the many shipwrecks that occurred here.

Wyman: Some of the earliest settlers of the town were named Wyman. The lake that is part of the Kennebec River is named for a former president of Central Maine Power, Walter Wyman. The dam that created this lake is named for him as well.

Wytopitlock: Abenaki for "at the place where there are alders."

Y

Yankeetuladi: This is a hybrid name combing the English "Yankee" with the Malecite word meaning "place where they make canoes." The word "Yankee" has an interesting origin. The Dutch originally settled the New York City area, and many of them didn't like the English who began to settle there. They had a derogatory name for the English: Jan (pronounced "yawn") Cheese. It evolved into "Yankee" and became a name of pride for Americans.

Yarmouth: Yarmouth was part of North Yarmouth until 1849 when it was incorporated as a separate town. North Yarmouth was named after Yarmouth, England and North was added to its name to differentiate it from Yarmouth, Massachusetts. When Yarmouth was split off in 1849, the differentiation was no longer needed, as Maine was no longer part of Massachusetts. The island and other sites have the same origin.

Yoke Ponds: Named because they look like an ox-yoke.

York: The Abenaki called this area Agamenticus, which means "the other side of the little river" or "the little river which hides behind an island in its mouth." The Pilgrims, who had rights to trade in parts of Maine, built a trading post here and called it by the Indian name. Sir Ferdinando Gorges later established a town calling it Agamenticus. Gorges changed the charter so that the town could become a city and the name was changed to Gorgeana in 1642. It was the first city in English, North America. Massachusetts, claiming it owned Maine, changed the name to York in 1652 when it was incorporated, wanting no acknowledgement of Gorges' claims. The name comes from York, England. York was destroyed during the French and Indian War with many settlers killed and 73 women and children taken to Canada by the Indians. The York Sons of Liberty had their own Tea Party during the Revolution, but the tea was never dumped in the harbor. It just disappeared, causing many to think the colonists used it. York County was created in 1735.

York Island: Benjamin York settled this island off Isle au Haut.

Z

Zion Hill: Named for the Biblical Zion.

Zircon Mountain: This site and others around it are named for the zircon stones found there.

BIBLIOGRAPHY

The detailed bibliography can be found on the book's website: www.thenamesofmaine.com